Listening All Night to the Rain

Listening All Night to the Rain

SELECTED POEMS OF SU DONGPO (SU SHI)

林下對床聽夜雨：
蘇東坡 (蘇軾) 詩選英譯 / 林健一，楊大維

Bilingual Edition

TRANSLATED BY JIANN I. LIN AND DAVID YOUNG

PINYON PUBLISHING
Montrose, Colorado

Many thanks to Richard K. Kent for his careful readings of the manuscript.

Cover Art "Near Guilin, Guangxi Province, China" by William L. Fink

Design by Susan Entsminger

First Hardcover Edition: May 2020

Pinyon Publishing
23847 V66 Trail, Montrose, CO 81403
www.pinyon-publishing.com

Library of Congress Control Number: 2020933013
ISBN: 978-1-936671-65-6

CONTENTS

II 1076-1079

III 1080-1089

IV 1090-1101

V POEMS OF UNCERTAIN DATE

SU DONGPO: AN INTRODUCTION

A thousand years separate us from this poet, and yet his voice, despite large differences of language, culture, and geography, feels fresh, immediate, and intimate. That is partly an eloquent testimony to the power of poetry to overcome time and change. Certain aspects of human experience are universal; a good poet understands that and can use it to advantage.

Moreover, the tradition within which Su Dongpo wrote featured a poetics and an aesthetic that combined simplicity with universality, but also left room for genius: many poets from the period in which he lived, the Song dynasty (960-1279), are no longer read or admired, while Su Shi (1037-1101), better known by his literary name, Su Dongpo, has been rightly cherished as one of China's greatest poets, keeping company with earlier Tang dynasty (618-907) masters like Wang Wei, Du Fu, and Li Bai.

"Dongpo" means "eastern slope" and reflects a bitter exile to a remote province as punishment for his political affiliations. It was a time of upheavals; one day his party might be in power and he could enjoy a high post in the capital; next they might be disgraced and he would experience prison and ever more distant provincial banishments. That he kept his high spirits intact through all those fluctuations of fortune is one reflection of his greatness and durability. Self-pity was off the table. Life was too interesting to be spoiled by adversities and adversaries; better to seek out whatever might sustain and nourish one's sense of wonder and delight. That at least is the major impulse behind his poems. Daoism and Chan (Zen) Buddhism helped show the way and reinforce the poetic sensibility.

1

The traveling necessitated by the exiles and banishments led to discoveries of places, people, and circumstances the poet would otherwise never have known. Making new friends, exploring remote temples, climbing rugged mountains, sharing poems over wine, Su Dongpo is almost always in a posture of discovery and modest celebration. Of course, sometimes it rains too much, or he misses his brother; the seasons can be harsh, and having to uproot and move is always distressing. But the poet is ready, right up to the end of his life, for the next pleasure and the next poem. Our privilege is to share them.

Delight is not always the mood of the poet, however. Su Dongpo is emotionally candid in the extreme, which means that he will not sidestep pain, loss, separation, or distress. Here, for example, is his famous account of dreaming about his dead wife, old grief bursting afresh, nothing held back:

A dream of my dead wife

To the tune, 'Of Jinling'

Ten years gone
　　　here in the dark I feel the miserable loss

I have tried not to think of it
　　　but it is unforgettable

her lone grave a thousand miles away
        nobody there to tell her story.

If we saw each other now
        she probably wouldn't recognize me

my face is dusty and dirty
        my hair has gotten gray

tonight in my dream
        I was back in our sweet hometown

I glanced in the small pavilion window
        she was dressing and putting on makeup

we gazed at each other, speechless,
        tears streaming down our faces

I know it's the tenth anniversary
        of heartbreak and separation

I picture the family plot on the pine ridge
        deserted in brilliant moonlight.

He had married Wang Fu (1039-1065) when she was fifteen and she had died at twenty-six. Ten years later, in 1075, he had this dream and wrote this poem. Its simplicity and sorrow are unforgettable.

Su Dongpo's brother, Su Zhe (1039-1112), also a poet, was someone else he missed and longed for as their lives took them in separate directions. They exchanged poems, along with news and gossip, sharing their joys and difficulties. Here is Dongpo, late in life, writing one of many such letter/poem/tributes:

Thinking about my brother

The lamp drops cinders
    the darkening candle wick
        hangs down

I poke the ashes in the stove
    over and over
        sniffing the last fragrance

a fresh breeze comes
    a crow flies up among the trees
        soaring and wheeling

the waning moon begins to rise
    dogs bark
        clouds pass

I close my eyes
    I feel my heart
        I need to plan my life

I'm traipsing after
    my own shadow
        longing for my oldest friend

while he, the magistrate
    may also be sitting up
        anxious, longing for me

across the sea between us
    the moon shines clear as crystal
        I share it with him now.

The full title of this poem from 1097 is something like "On the 17th day of the 12th month, sitting up all night until dawn (while cherishing the memory of my brother) this poem is to express my feelings for Ziyou (i.e., Su Zhe)." Details that are apparently casually selected – the lamp and candle, the ashes in the stove, the soaring crow, the moonrise and barking dogs – all work beautifully to establish the mixed feelings of love and sorrow that the poet is experiencing, a map of his emotional landscape, while the final image of moon and sea helps to resolve his dilemma, for the present at least. The poem stands in for the absence and presence of the two poet-brothers. And it's interesting that both of the poems I've quoted, different as they are, close with the calming image of moonlight, a trope that had originated years earlier in Du Fu's love poem to his absent wife during the Tang dynasty (618-907). That moon, we suddenly realize, is the same one we see now.

If poems can be letters, they can also be texts to accompany landscape paintings, inscriptions for temple walls, and commemorations of excursions and drinking parties. This helps explain the prolific output of Su Dongpo – something like 2,400 poems – and it constitutes a warning about our selection: we have not tried to represent the formal variety of this poet, but have rather chosen poems we especially enjoy, most frequently in the four-line, seven-character per line lyric that allowed him both expressiveness and economy. These quatrains could easily double in size, to eight lines, or vary their line length to five syllables. What we have not undertaken are the prose poems or the ci, poems fitted to well-known melodies (with one exception, #32, quoted above).

If economy was a hallmark of the lyric, that rule did not extend to titles, which were often documentations of time, place, obligation, and circumstance. We have used the notes to translate the titles more fully and encourage readers to explore them in order to inhabit Su Dongpo's world more fully, as appropriate.

Readers wishing to know more about the poet's life can consult the strange and lively biography by Lin Yutang, *The Gay Genius* (1947, before "gay" carried its current connotations). Those wishing for more examples of his poetry can find them in anthologies like Robert Payne's *The White Pony* (1947), Kenneth Rexroth's *100 Poems from the Chinese* (1956), and David Hinton's remarkable *Classical Chinese Poetry* (2008) and his *Mountain Home: The Wilderness Poetry of Ancient China* (2002, 2005). A book-length selection by the late Burton Watson, *Selected Poems of Su Tung-p'o* (1994), is extremely rewarding, both for its scholarship and quality of translations. While it has some overlap with our own selection, we regard it as a complementary volume rather than a rival.

This is the third such collaboration between Lin and Young —the others were *The Clouds Float North: the Complete Poems of Yu Xuanji* (Wesleyan, 1998) and *Out on the Autumn River: Selected Poems of Du Mu* (RagerMedia, 2007). It represents many years of careful study and discussion. Jiann Lin provides the literal, character-by-character versions; David Young shapes them into poems in English; we then discuss and agree on final versions. Creativity and scholarship are factors throughout the process and collaboration is something we think our Chinese subjects would have understood and approved of. While our portrait of Su Dongpo is partial and selective, given his enormous output, we like to hope that it goes to the very heart of his accomplishment as a poet.

David Young
Oberlin, Ohio
May, 2019

I
1059–1075

1. 牛口見月

掩窗寂已睡
月腳垂孤光
披衣起周覽
飛露灑我裳
山川同一色
浩若涉大荒
幽懷耿不寐
四顧獨徬徨
忽憶丙申年
京邑大雨霶
蔡河中夜決
橫浸國南方
車馬無復見
紛紛操桄郎
新秋忽已晴
九陌尚汪洋
龍津觀夜市
燈火亦煌煌
新月皎如晝
疏星弄寒芒

1. Watching the moon after coming by boat to Niukou Island

Sleepy, closing the windows for the night,
I glimpse the setting moon,

throw on a wrap, wakeful, and go outside.
The dew dampens my robe,

and the countryside is all one color,
stretching away like a wilderness.

Sleepless and filled with emotion,
I gaze around, lonely, hesitant,

and suddenly recall, three years ago,
the great rainstorm at the capital

when the river burst its banks
flooding the countryside to the south

clearing the roads of carts and horses,
no way to travel but bamboo rafts, ferrymen busy,

and autumn came and the sky cleared,
but still the roads were under water –

though the night market at Longjin Bridge thrived
shining with bright lanterns

and the young moon was bright as daytime,
and stars were scattered, their cool rays playing,

不知京國喧
謂是江湖鄉
今來牛口渚
見月重淒涼
却思舊遊處
滿陌沙塵黃

and I wasn't aware of national upheavals
and felt at home wherever I went.

Now, ferried to this island,
seeing the moon renews my desolation

and sends me back to those earlier scenes
and the clouds of yellow dust along the roads.

2. 江上看山

船上看山如走馬
倏忽過去數百羣
前山槎牙忽變態
後嶺雜沓如驚奔
仰看微徑斜繚繞
上有行人高縹緲
舟中舉手欲與言
孤帆南去如飛鳥

2. Looking up at mountains from the river

Aboard the ferry, watching mountains,
    like galloping on horseback,
we seem to pass groups of a hundred or more,
    in an eye-blink.

The mountains ahead change postures,
    like wood cut at a slant,
and the peaks behind look disordered,
    frightened, running away.

If you look up you can make out
    winding trails leading up,
and people walking the high ridge,
    barely visible in mist.

I wave from our boat
    wishing we could converse,
from this lone sailing junk,
    flying south like a bird.

3. 望夫臺

山頭孤石遠亭亭
江轉船回石似屏
可憐千古長如昨
船去船來自不停
浩浩長江赴滄海
紛紛過客似浮萍
誰能坐待山月出
照見寒影高伶俜

3. The Waiting-for-Husband Terrace

She's a lonely stone outcrop near the peak,
    tall and erect in the distance.

The river winds past, boats come and go;
    the stone stands like a screen.

Pity that lasts forever, time's slow crawl,
    day after endless day,

boats heading upriver, downriver,
    a procession with no end.

The Yangtze, so gigantic,
    bound for the blue ocean,

travelers passing, passing,
    like so much drifting duckweed.

How could she sit so quietly
    and wait for the mountain moonrise,

among cold shadows like a light
    high up and all alone?

4. 昭君村

昭君本楚人
豔色照江水
楚人不敢娶
謂是漢妃子
誰知去鄉國
萬里為胡鬼
人言生女作門楣
昭君當時憂色衰
古來人事盡如此
反覆縱橫安可知

4. At Princess Zhaojun's village

Zhaojun was originally
  from Chu State

they say her dazzling beauty
  mirrored the flowing river

people from Chu
  didn't dare to marry her

they knew she was a concubine
  of the Han imperial court –

who knew that she would leave
  her home country

and journey a thousand miles
  sent to the king of Xiongnu?

People hope their baby girls
  might bring the family wealth and fame

she had to worry constantly
  about keeping her good looks

that's how human affairs have gone
  since time immemorial

we scheme but never can be sure
  about the outcome.

5. 和子由澠池懷舊

人生到處知何似
應似飛鴻踏雪泥
泥上偶然留指爪
鴻飛那復計東西
老僧已死成新塔
壞壁無由見舊題
往日崎嶇還記否
路長人困蹇驢嘶

5. Poem in reply to my brother's poem of nostalgia for Mianchi

Who can say how life should look?
We are like swans that walk on slushy snow,

leaving their muddy footprints,
and, when they soar, go off in what direction?

The old monks died, the new pagoda's built,
ruined walls and old inscriptions vanish.

Then why do we still recall the tumult,
long roads, exhausted travelers, crippled braying donkeys?

6. 柳

今年手自栽
問我何年去
他年我復來
搖落傷人意

6. The willow tree

This year I plant it myself,
    using my own hands.

Somebody asked me what year
    I went away?

Another year,
    and I came back again.

The little tree waves and shakes,
    same as my hurting heart.

7. 題寶雞縣斯飛閣

西南歸路遠蕭條
倚檻魂飛不可招
野闊牛羊同雁鶩
天長草樹接雲霄
昏昏水氣浮山麓
泛泛春風弄麥苗
誰使愛官輕去國
此身無計老漁樵

7. Inscribed on a fancy pavilion in Shaanxi

Given the distance,
　　it's hard to imagine
　　　　traveling all the way home.

I lean on the railing,
　　my spirit flies away,
　　　　and I can't call it back.

It crosses a vast wilderness,
　　herds of sheep and cattle,
　　　　flocks of geese and ducks.

The sky is high overhead,
　　but the trees and bushes
　　　　reach up to try and touch it.

The murky water
　　laps around
　　　　the mountain's feet.

A nervous spring breeze
　　drifts among
　　　　the sprouting wheat.

Those who seek office
　　are fools to leave
　　　　their native haunts.

Here at my wit's end,
　　I'll just turn common,
　　　　an old woodcutter ... or a fisherman.

8. 扶風天和寺

遠望若可愛
朱欄碧瓦溝
聊為一駐足
且慰百回頭
水落見山石
塵高昏市樓
臨風莫長嘯
遺響浩難收

8. At the Celestial Harmony Temple in Shaanxi

It looks so lovely
    there in the distance,

vermilion balustrades,
    green glazed drain tiles.

I've climbed up
    to pay a quick visit

often turning to look,
    taking comfort in the view,

waterfalls and cliffs,
    rockfaces,

some dust floats up
    dimming the city and its markets.

I face into the wind,
    no need to try and shout –

it makes a noise so vast
    it's out of my control.

9. 綠筠亭

愛竹能延客
求詩剩掛牆
風梢千畝亂
月影萬夫長
谷鳥驚棋響
山蜂識酒香
只應陶靖節
會聽北窗涼

9. Green Bamboo Pavilion

This place attracts
  many lovers of bamboo.

Celebrities are asked for poems
  to frame and hang on walls.

Winds blow the tops of bamboo trees
  and the leaves wave like warrior banners;

dim moonlight covers the bamboo trees
  a tall, luxuriant army.

The valley birds are roused
  by our shouts as we play chess;

the mountain bees are drawn
  by the odor of our wine.

I think of the poet-recluse
  known as Tao Qian,

and understand his pleasure
  sleeping in cool air next to a window.

10. 出都來陳，所乘
船上有題小詩八首，
不知何人有感於余心
者，聊為和之 (其三)

烟火動村落

晨光尚熹微

田園處處好

淵明胡不歸

10. Response to a poem found in a boat

Smoke from a few kitchen fires,
    the villages are stirring.

Dawn's on the way, still just
    a few faint rays.

I love this rural scenery
    a place any wise man

would be happy
    to call home.

11. 出潁口初見淮山，是日至壽州

我行日夜向江海

楓葉蘆花秋興長

長淮忽迷天遠近

青山久與船低昂

壽州已見白石塔

短棹未轉黃毛岡

波平風軟望不到

故人久立烟蒼茫

11. Traveling between provinces

Reassigned, I'm heading toward the sea,
    traveling by night and day.

Red maple leaves, white catkins,
    an autumn of emotions.

Out on the great Huai River,
    the world gets lost in mist.

Green mountains in the distance,
    bobbing as the boat sails past.

As we come to Shouzhou
    I can see the white stone pagoda.

Our small boat sails around
    hillocks of yellow thatch grass.

Calm waves, soft wind,
    no sign of my good friend,

is he waiting for me up ahead
    standing in hazy twilight?

12. 臘日遊孤山訪惠勤惠思二僧

天欲雪

雲滿湖

樓臺明滅山有無

水清石出魚可數

林深無人鳥相呼

臘日不歸對妻孥

名尋道人實自娛

道人之居在何許

12. Visiting two monks on a winter day

Snow clouds
  fill the sky
    and gather in the lake.

Houses and galleries.
  sometimes in view, sometimes hidden
    among the mountain shadows.

Clear water –
  lots of rocks
    and I can count the fish.

The forest is so deep
  nobody goes in there
    except for the birds, calling.

It's Winter Sacrifice Day
  and I should be back home
    facing my wife and children.

I say I'm searching for the Daoist priests
  but in reality
    it's for my own entertainment.

Where is their house
  and what does it look like,
    I ask myself.

寶雲山前路盤紆

孤山孤絕誰肯廬

道人有道山不孤

紙窗竹屋深自暖

擁褐坐睡依團蒲

天寒路遠愁僕夫

整駕催歸及未晡

出山回望雲木合

Ahead of me stands
    Treasure Cloud Mountain
        with all its twisting trails.

And Lone Mountain
    so isolated and deserted –
        who'd build a cottage here?

But when a Daoist finds perfection
    he's not alone,
        nor is the mountain.

Paper windows
    a bamboo hut
        full of warm, deep feelings.

Wrapped in coarse clothes
    sitting and sleeping
        on rush mats and rough cushions.

Cold weather plus
    a journey of such length –
        my servant worries.

Now he must find a carriage
    to get me home
        while it's still light out.

Leaving the mountain
    I turn to look back, admiring
        the mix of clouds and trees,

但見野鶻盤浮圖
茲遊淡薄歡有餘
到家恍如夢蘧蘧
作詩火急追亡逋
清景一失後難摹

and pause to watch
    a pair of wild falcons
        circling a pagoda.

This trip may not amount to much
    but the pleasure it has given me
        is plentiful.

And as I get back home
    the whole thing seems
        a kind of vivid dream

so I hasten to make this poem,
    to catch the images
        before they dissipate.

Once you lose them
    it's twice as hard
        to get them back again.

13. 吉祥寺僧求閣名

過眼榮枯電與風，
久長那得似花紅。
上人宴坐觀空閣，
觀色觀空色即空。

13. At a temple, asked to help name a pavilion

Glory will flourish and decay
    as transitory
        as any wind or thunder.

What lasts can be
    as simple as
        red blooming flowers.

The master priest sits quietly
    watching an empty shelf
        thinking about a name,

observing the concept of "real"
    and also the concept of "nothingness"
        because they're both the same.

14. 雨中遊天竺靈感觀音院

蠶欲老

麥半黃

前山後山雨浪浪

農夫輟耒女廢筐

白衣仙人在高堂

14. At a temple in the mountains, during rain

The silkworms are aging,
    the wheat is ripening, yellow,

the mountains ahead and behind
    are filled with surging rainstorms.

Farmers leave their plows,
    farm women stow their baskets

but the Goddess of Mercy, white-robed,
    still reigns here in her shrine.

15. 夜泛西湖五絕 (其二)

三更向闌月漸垂

欲落未落景特奇

明朝人事誰料得

看到蒼龍西沒時

15. Floating at night on West Lake (2nd of 5)

Perfect stillness
   deep night
      waning moonlight –

the moon has almost set
   which makes the light
      especially strange and wonderful

morning comes soon
   who can predict
      the news it brings?

Still, I got to see
   the black dragon constellation
      setting in the west.

16. 望海樓晚景五絕（其四）

樓下誰家燒夜香
玉笙哀怨弄初涼
臨風有客吟秋扇
拜月無人見晚粧

16. Night view at Ocean-Gazing Pavilion (4th of 5)

What family
   downstairs
      is burning nightly incense?

Someone else is playing
   a flute, sad music
      that fills the cool of evening.

Yet another visitor
   facing into the autumn wind
      is chanting a poem on a fan.

We all try to worship the moon
   but none of us seem to get
      a clear view of her beauty.

17. 梵天寺見僧守詮
小詩清婉可愛，次韻

但聞烟外鐘

不見烟中寺

幽人行未已

草露濕芒屨

惟應山頭月

夜夜照來去

17. Written to match a Chan (Zen) priest's poem

I can hear the bell's sound
    through the smoke

but I can't see
    the temple through the mist.

The lonely traveler
    walks and walks –

the dewy grass will soak
    his straw sandals

the glow behind the mountain
    can only be the rising moon –

night after night it shines
    as travelers come and go.

18. 祥符寺九曲觀燈

紗籠擎燭逢門入
銀葉燒香見客邀
金鼎轉丹光吐夜
寶珠穿蟻鬧連朝
波翻焰裏元相激
魚舞湯中不畏焦
明日酒醒空想像
清吟半逐夢魂銷

18. Enjoying the lanterns at Lucky Charm Temple

A silk-draped lantern
　　raised high, its candle light
　　　　leaking through door cracks

and the mangrove leaves
　　burning with incense
　　　　welcoming visitors.

These lanterns are golden cauldrons
　　transforming pellets
　　　　pouring out light in the darkness

like precious pearls
　　like busy ants
　　　　carrying night into morning,

waves of light, rolling in fire,
　　bouncing around,
　　　　colliding –

fish in hot water
　　swimming and dancing
　　　　unafraid of the heat …

We'll sober up
　　tomorrow
　　　　leave the whole day empty

chanting our poems
　　chasing a dream life
　　　　utterly happy.

19. 飲湖上初晴後雨二首 (其二)

水光瀲灧晴方好

山色空濛雨亦奇

若把西湖比西子

淡粧濃抹總相宜

19. Drinking on West Lake, clear first, then rain (2nd of 2)

The huge expanse of water
    ripples and shines
        all of a piece in sunlight

but the mist-shrouded hills
    on a rainy day
        are equally wonderful.

We can liken West Lake
    to Lady Xi Shi
        that great beauty:

whatever she wore,
    light makeup, or heavy,
        always, always attractive!

20. 新城道中二首（其一）

東風知我欲山行

吹斷簷間積雨聲

嶺上晴雲披絮帽

樹頭初日掛銅鉦

野桃含笑竹籬短

溪柳自搖沙水清

西崦人家應最樂

煮芹燒筍餉春耕

20. On the road to Xincheng (1st of 2)

The east wind seems to know
    I'm setting out
        on mountain roads –

it blows away
    the excess rain
        dripping from the eaves.

Above the mountain range
    clouds like cotton wadding
        against a clear blue sky –

over the treetops
    the rising sun
        hangs like a bronze gong.

Peach trees in open fields
    smiling, blossoming
        beyond the bamboo fence –

willows by a sandy stream
    waving freely
        as the water clears.

Families off to the west
    part of the sunset
        ought to be happy,

cooking their celery and parsley
    adding fresh bamboo shoots,
        treating their visitors to spring vegetables.

21. 山村五絕 (其一)

竹籬茅屋趁溪斜
春入山村處處花
無象太平還有象
孤烟起處是人家

21. In a mountain village (1st of 5)

A bamboo fence
    thatched cottages
        along the tumbling stream

spring is arriving
    in this mountain village
        flowers blossoming everywhere –

peace and prosperity
    are pretty hard to find
        this isn't the best of times –

but here in the back country
    where lonely smoke is rising
        ordinary people live their lives.

22. 於潛僧綠筠軒

可使食無肉
不可使居無竹
無肉令人瘦
無竹令人俗
人瘦尚可肥
俗士不可醫
旁人笑此言
似高還似癡
若對此君仍大嚼
世間那有揚州鶴

58

22. Encountering a monk near his temple

It's fine to eat meals
    without meat

but a place without bamboo groves
    is out of the question –

going without meat
    can make you thin

but having no bamboo around
    will make you vulgar –

a thin person
    can be fattened up

but vulgarity
    can't be cured.

People laugh at me
    for saying this

they think I make too much
    of the nobility of bamboo

but if you ever have to choose
    between great food and mere bamboo

choose the bamboo
    and your dreams will come true!

23. 陌上花三首 (其一)

陌上花開蝴蝶飛
江山猶是昔人非
遺民幾度垂垂老
遊女長歌緩緩歸

23. Roadside flowers (1st of 3)

Flowers blooming in the fields,
   along the roads,
      butterflies everywhere

the land and nation stay the same –
   change involves the people
      how they come and go

all the great upheavals
   and their few survivors
      reaching a high old age …

daughters marry and travel far
   chanting a long long time
      "no hurry, but do come home."

24. 九日，尋臻闍黎，遂泛小舟至勤師院，二首 (其二)

湖上青山翠作堆

蔥蔥鬱鬱氣佳哉

笙歌叢裏抽身出

雲水光中洗眼來

白足赤髭迎我笑

拒霜黃菊為誰開

明年桑苧煎茶處

憶著袁翁首重回

24. The Double Ninth Festival, a visit by boat to two priests (2nd of 2)

Out on the lake
   hills fresh and green
      blue mountains piled beyond

green in every direction
   life is good
      loaded with beauty and welcome

I barely got away
   from all the singing and dancing
      I was involved in

to join this vivid scenery
   become a part of
      the clouds, the water, the light.

Two monks
   Cleanfoot and Redbeard
      welcome me with smiles

the rose hibiscus
   the yellow chrysanthemum
      they bloom for whom?

Next year, Double Ninth,
   here where an old man
      made brick tea

remember my promise
   this old guy
      will visit you again!

25. 書雙竹湛師房二首（其一）

我本西湖一釣舟

意嫌高屋冷颼颼

羨師此室繞方丈

一炷清香盡日留

25. Written in praise of a monk's cell (1st of 2)

First of all, I'm like a boat
    floating along
        on West Lake

wanting to avoid
    the grand houses of the rich –
        I find them cold.

I envy this monk's room
    a small space
        just a few square feet

one stick of incense
    makes it fragrant
        all the day long.

26. 遊鶴林、招隱二首（其二）

行歌白雲嶺

坐詠修竹林

風輕花自落

日薄山半陰

澗草誰復識

聞香杳難尋

時見城市人

幽居惜未深

26. Touring two temples (2nd of 2)

Walking the mountain ridges
   singing among white clouds

sitting down and chanting
   among the tall bamboo

the wind blows softly
   flower petals fall

sun going down
   the mountain half in shadow.

Who else would know
   these mountain torrent grasses

or trace their fragrance
   distant and elusive?

Now and then I glimpse
   some city folks

glad that I live secluded
   though not secluded enough.

27. 常潤道中，有懷錢塘，寄述古五首（其二）

草長江南鶯亂飛

年來事事與心違

花開後院還空落

燕入華堂怪未歸

世上功名何日是

樽前點檢幾人非

去年柳絮飛時節

記得金籠放雪衣

27. Sent to a friend (2nd of 5)

High grass in the Yangtze delta
  large flocks of orioles

events of recent years have gone
  contrary to my heart.

Flowers bloom in the back yard
  all of them will wither

swallows fly out of a mansion
  my fault I can't go home

will the day come in this world
  when ambition and merit are one?

Sitting in front of the wine jar
  discussing other people's wrongs

last year at this time
  willow catkins were blowing around

and I remember white doves
  freed from their golden dovecote.

28. 青牛嶺高絕處，有小寺，人迹罕到

暮歸走馬沙河塘

爐烟裊裊十里香

朝行曳杖青牛嶺

寒泉咽咽千山靜

君勿笑老僧

耳聾喚不聞

百年俱是可憐人

明朝且復城中去

28. The temple on Black Ox Ridge

Trotting on horseback
   coming back to Sand River Dyke
      in deepening dusk

the incense smoke curls upward
   I catch its fragrance
      even ten miles away

on my morning walk
   dragging a stick
      I head toward Black Ox Ridge

as spring, still cold, seems to whimper
   surrounded by
      a thousand silent mountains –

Gentlemen,
   don't poke fun
      at this old monk,

he's kind of hard of hearing
   and wouldn't
      catch your drift,

all his life
   he's been
      a pitiable creature

tomorrow I have to go back
   and re-enter
      the bustling city

白雲却在題詩處

leaving white clouds behind
where I stayed
and wrote this poem.

29. 出城送客，不及，步至溪上，二首（其一）

送客客已去

尋花花未開

未能城裏去

且復水邊來

父老借問我

使君安在哉

今年好雨雪

會見麥千堆

29. Saying goodbye to a friend (1st of 2)

I came to see my friend leave
    and he's already gone

we search around for flowers
    but they aren't blooming yet

I can't go straight to find him
    because of the city wall

but I can go around
    and meet him by the river

elders may stop me there
    to ask me

where they can find
    the honorable governor

the growing season's been good
    favorable snow and rainfall

which led to this great harvest
    a thousand mounds of wheat.

30. 和子由四首
（其二：送春）

夢裏青春可得追

欲將詩句絆餘暉

酒闌病客惟思睡

蜜熟黃蜂亦懶飛

芍藥櫻桃俱掃地

鬢絲禪榻兩忘機

憑君借取法界觀

一洗人間萬事非

30. Poem in answer to my brother (2nd of 4)

My younger days
   come back to me
      in dreams

I'd like to have my poems
   capture the light
      arrest the sunset

my drinking friends are gone
   leaving this sick man, me,
      in need of sleep

the honey is ripe
   the wasps
      too lazy to fly

the peonies
   are withered
      likewise the cherries

my hair's gone grey
   I sit on my meditation couch
      trying to forget age and sickness

I want you to lend me
   a copy of your
      Buddhist mantra

Once and for all
   I'll wash out things
      that have to do with wrong and evil.

31. 小兒

小兒不識愁
起坐牽我衣
我欲嗔小兒
老妻勸兒癡
兒癡君更甚
不樂愁何為
還坐愧此言
洗盞當我前
大勝劉伶婦
區區為酒錢

31. My little child

My little boy
   careless and uninhibited

runs wild in our house
   grabbing at my clothes

I start to scold him
   for the way he's acting

but my wife reminds me
   he's just having fun

"If he is silly, husband,
   you might be even sillier,

you need to cheer up
   stop being so serious!"

Back at my desk
   I am abashed

she washes some cups
   and serves me wine

way better than that wife
   of olden times

who wouldn't let her husband drink
   because it was expensive.

32. 江城子（乙卯正月二十日夜記夢）

十年生死兩茫茫，

不思量，自難忘。

千里孤墳，無處話淒涼。

縱使相逢應不識，

塵滿面，鬢如霜。

夜來幽夢忽還鄉，

小軒窗，正梳妝。

相顧無言，惟有淚千行。

料得年年腸斷處，

明月夜，短松岡。

32. A dream of my dead wife

To the tune, 'Of Jinling'

Ten years gone
    here in the dark I feel the miserable loss

I have tried not to think of it
    but it is unforgettable

her lone grave a thousand miles away
    nobody there to tell her story.

If we saw each other now
    she probably wouldn't recognize me

my face is dusty and dirty
    my hair has gotten gray

tonight in my dream
    I was back in our sweet hometown

I glanced in the small pavilion window
    she was dressing and putting on makeup

we gazed at each other, speechless,
    tears streaming down our faces

I know it's the tenth anniversary
    of heartbreak and separation

I picture the family plot on the pine ridge
    deserted in brilliant moonlight.

II

1076–1079

33. 和文與可洋川園池三十首 · 露香亭 (其十六)

亭下佳人錦繡衣

滿身瓔珞綴明璣

晚香消歇無尋處

花已飄零露已晞

33. Another poem for Wen Tong and his gardens (16th of 30)

There's an attractive young lady
    by the pavilion
        dressed in gorgeous brocades

wearing a splendid necklace
    and other jewelry
        including some brilliant pearls

the evening fragrance of the tuberoses
    disperses quickly
        until you can't detect it

the flowers fade and fall
    the morning dew dries up
        fast in the rising sun.

34. 登常山絕頂廣麗亭

西望穆陵關

東望瑯邪臺

南望九仙山

北望空飛埃

相將叫虞舜

遂欲歸蓬萊

嗟我二三子

狂飲亦荒哉

紅裙欲仙去

長笛有餘哀

34. Climbing Mount Chang to visit the temple

I look west
    toward the Pass

I look east
    at the terrace

I look south
    to the mountain

I look north
    at the dust clouds

they make me recall
    the ancient Emperor

and wish I could visit
    the mountain fairyland.

Alas, two or three of you,
    my companions,

our outrageous drinking,
    isn't it strange?

The red-skirted beauty
    turns into a fairy

the long flute carries
    a lasting note of sadness

清歌入雲霄，
妙舞纖腰回。
自從有此山，
白石封蒼苔。
何嘗有此樂，
將去復徘徊。
人生如朝露，
白髮日夜催。
棄置當何言，
萬劫終飛灰。

we hear quiet singing
    music rising to the skies

we watch the slender dancers
    whirling and circling.

Ever since there's been
    a mountain,

white stone
    wrapped in green moss,

hasn't there always been
    this kind of pleasure?

Leaving, I find myself
    pacing up and down –

life is like the morning dew
    fading fast

white hair overtakes us
    pressing day and night.

Let it go, friends,
    what else is there to say?

Everything eventually
    will turn to blowing ashes.

35. 同年王中甫挽詞

先帝親收十五人
四方爭看擊鵬鷃
如君事業真堪用
顧我衰遲不足論
出處升沉十年後
死生契闊幾人存
他時京口尋遺跡
宿草猶應有淚痕

35. Eulogy for Wang

The late Emperor
  personally sought out
    fifteen geniuses

and people from all quarters
  watched and applauded
    these men of great achievement.

Your career
  matched expectations,
    made all kinds of sense,

while mine, I fear,
  feeble, declining,
    is not worth a mention.

To enter the government,
  to rise and fall in favor
    decade after decade,

life and death,
  meeting and parting,
    how do friendships survive?

When I can travel
  to Jiangsu Province
    in search of history

I will seek out your tomb
  covered with old grass
    still traced with tears.

36. 和孔密州五絕：
東欄梨花（其三）

梨花淡白柳深青

柳絮飛時花滿城

惆悵東欄二株雪

人生看得幾清明

36. Pear blossom poem for Kong (3rd of 5)

The flowering pear trees
   are like white frost
      the willows a deep green

willow catkins
   float past
      flowers fill the city

I have a sense of sadness
   that comes from watching
      a couple of snowy pear trees –

how many Qing Ming festivals
   are left for me to witness
      in this brief lifetime?

37. 陽關詞三首·中秋月（其三）

暮雲收盡溢清寒

銀漢無聲轉玉盤

此生此夜不長好

明月明年何處看

37. Sun Gate Pass (3rd of 3)

Evening, sunset,
   clouds at the horizon
      an overflowing sense of cold

the Milky Way roams silently
   and the moon's a jade plate
      rising and growing bright

Moonfest days in my lifetime
   don't always have clear nights
      when we can view

tonight the moon is bright
   I can be with my brother –
      But where will we be next year?

38.《虔州八境圖》八首，並引（其七）

雲烟縹緲鬱孤臺

積翠浮空雨半開

想見之罘觀海市

絳宮明滅是蓬萊

38. Qianzhou scenes (7th of 8)

A misty fog
    and I can hardly see
        Yugu Pavilion

luxuriant grass
    trees floating in air
        a light rain

feels like I'm on
    a mythical island
        inside a mirage

the crimson palace of the gods
    comes and goes in the mist
        along with the magic mountain.

39. 觀子美病中作，嗟歎不足，因次韻

百尺長松澗下摧，

知君此意為誰來。

霜枝半折孤根出，

尚有狂風急雨催。

39. For Zimei, on his being sick

A hundred foot pine
   can snap in half
      under a mountain torrent

I know, my friend,
   about your illness
      and what makes you write.

Here is a frosted twig, half broken,
   or an exposed
      lonely root

and still the storm continues
   the wind and driving rains
      urging us on.

40. 九日次韻王鞏

我醉欲眠君罷休
已教從事到青州
鬢霜饒我三千丈
詩律輸君一百籌
聞道郎君閉東閣
且容老子上南樓
相逢不用忙歸去
明日黃花蝶也愁

40. For Wang Gong, on the Double Ninth Festival

I'm drunk and sleepy
   and you, my friend,
      are resting at your ease

you have a government position
   thus you can enjoy
      fine wine

my hair is frosted white
   around the temples
      and has gotten very long

and as for poems
   you're way ahead of me
      in composition

I hear my noble lord
   has closed his guest rooms
      no more visitors

why don't we two old guys
   climb together
      to the south pavilion

we've just begun
   to get to know each other
      no need to rush back

when things go out of date
   even the butterflies
      get depressing.

41. 李思訓畫《長江絕島圖》

山蒼蒼

水茫茫

大孤小孤江中央

崖崩路絕猿鳥去

惟有喬木攙天長

客舟何處來

棹歌中流聲抑揚

沙平風軟望不到

41. Inscription for a landscape painting

Mountains
    green and azure

river waters
    boundless

the great lone mountain
    and the smaller one
        both stand mid-river

cliffs that become landslides
    inaccessible roads
        only birds and monkeys

nothing but tall, stately trees
    reaching high
        toward the sky.

That passenger boat
    where is it coming from?

They are singing boat-songs
    there in mid-river
        cadences rise and fall

soft winds
    blow invisibly
        over the flat sandbanks

孤山久與船低昂

峨峨兩烟鬟

曉鏡開新粧

舟中賈客莫漫狂

小姑前年嫁彭郎

the islands have been here
   a long long time, watching
      boats rise and fall, come and go.

Both mountains resemble
   well-dressed beauties
      with gorgeous hairdos

sitting at their mirrors
   freshening their makeup
      getting dressed

you merchants, in those boats,
   don't get flirtatious
      and unruly

the young lady, just last year,
   already married
      a young man named Peng-rock.

42. 登雲龍山

醉中走上黃茅岡
滿岡亂石如群羊
岡頭醉倒石作床
仰看白雲天茫茫
歌聲落谷秋風長
路人舉首東南望
拍手大笑使君狂

42. Climbing Dragon-Cloud Mountain

Drunk, I climbed up
   through yellow cogon grass
      to the high ridge

the scattered boulders
   around the ridge looked like
      a flock of grazing sheep

drunk, I lay down
   on a flat rock
      there on the hilltop

staring up
   at the boundless sky
      filled with white clouds

I could hear singing in the valley
   or was it the whistle
      of the autumn wind?

Some strangers came along
   craning their necks
      looking in all directions

they clapped and laughed
   at the sight
      of this bewildered bigwig.

43. 十月十五日觀月黃樓，席上次韻

中秋天氣未應殊

不用紅紗照座隅

山上白雲橫匹素

水中明月臥浮圖

未成短棹還三峽

已約輕舟泛五湖

為問登臨好風景

明年還憶使君無

43. Moon viewing at the Yellow Tower

Mid-autumn festival
   weather hasn't been
      too unusual

no need to use
   red gauze
      to decorate our seats

white clouds on the mountain
   crossing in a line
      like plain spun silk

bright moonlight
   reflected in the water
      Buddhist pagoda upside down

I'd like a little boat
   on which to sail
      back to the Three Gorges

but I already have one
   for drifting around
      in the lakes of the Delta

I might as well ask
   if it's fun to visit scenery
      admire landscapes

and if I left
   within a year
      who would remember this Magistrate?

44. 和田國博喜雪

疇昔月如晝

晚來雲暗天

玉花飛半夜

翠浪舞明年

螟螣無遺種

流亡稍占田

歲豐君不樂

鐘磬幾時編

44. Poem written on a snowy day

I'm remembering past days when
    the moon was bright as daylight

snow clouds at evening
    fill the darkening sky

pure snowflakes, jade flowers
    dancing until midnight

next year wheat will sprout
    wave after endless wave

the insects that devour it
    killed off in this snowfall

destitute peasants
    will have good land to farm.

In a former year of bumper crops
    you were still lost in mourning

let's look ahead for the right time
    to ring our bells and stones!

45. 月夜與客飲杏花下

杏花飛簾散餘春
明月入戶尋幽人
褰衣步月踏花影
炯如流水涵青蘋
花間置酒清香發
爭挽長條落香雪
山城酒薄不堪飲

45. Drinking in moonlight by the apricot orchard

Apricot trees
   and blowing curtains
      flavor of spring

moonlight enters
   like someone searching
      for solitude and scenery

lifting robes
   walking in the moonlight
      treading on flower shadows

everything clear
   as river water
      flowing above green weeds

wine and food set out
   near the blooming shrubs
      mix of pleasant odors

picking long twigs up
   from among
      white fallen flowers

here in the mountains
   our local wine
      may not be up to your standards

勸君且吸杯中月
洞簫聲斷月明中
惟憂月落酒杯空
明朝捲地春風惡
但見綠葉棲殘紅

but let yourself
    enjoy a cup
        that has been mixed with moonlight

sound of a bamboo flute
    suddenly goes silent
        in brilliant moonshine

our only worries?
    Moonset
        and empty cups

tomorrow morning
    wicked spring breezes
        will be kicking up

nothing to see
    but green leaves, covering
        faded and fallen flowers.

46. 雪上訪道人不遇

花光紅滿欄

草色綠無岸

不逢青眼人

長歌白石澗

46. Missing my meeting with a priest

Splendor of flowers
    filling the balustrades with red

grass in every shade of green
    along the endless shore

I couldn't find
    the amazing man I came to see

so I chanted some poems instead
    into the white mountain gully.

47. 予以事繫御史臺獄，獄吏稍見侵，自度不能堪，死獄中，不得一別子由，故和二詩授獄卒梁成，以遺子由，二首（其一）

聖主如天萬物春

小臣愚暗自亡身

百年未滿先償債

十口無歸更累人

是處青山可埋骨

他時夜雨獨傷神

與君今世為兄弟

又結來生未了因

47. From prison, to my brother (1st of 2)

Our Emperor, on high,
   favors all things on earth
      like spring's arrival

whereas I'm a minor official
   ignorant, obscure,
      who has wrecked his own life.

I won't reach a hundred years
   to pay my debts
      and clear my name

and ten people I support
   my family
      will become your burden.

Bury my bones
   anywhere you like
      among green hills.

It may pain you to remember
   long talks we had
      on rainy nights.

I was lucky, in this life,
   to have a brother
      noble as a prince

and our deep bond will stretch
   beyond my death
      into an unknown future.

III

1080–1089

48. 梅花二首 (其一)

春來幽谷水潺潺
的皪梅花草棘間
一夜東風吹石裂
半隨飛雪度關山

48. The plum trees (1st of 2)

Spring arrives
  a murmuring stream that flows
    through a deep secluded valley

plum blossoms stand out
  among thick grass
    thistles and thorns

then, overnight,
  the east winds blow
    cold enough to crack the rocks

and the blossoms float
  among the snowflakes
    crossing the forts and hills.

49. 初到黃州

自笑平生為口忙
老來事業轉荒唐
長江繞郭知魚美
好竹連山覺筍香
逐客不妨員外置
詩人例作水曹郎
只慚無補絲毫事
尚費官家壓酒囊

49. Arriving in Huangzhou for the first time

I have to laugh at myself
    busy all my life
        trying to support my family

and now, as I grow old,
    my whole career
        is turning idle, silly.

This place, my new assignment,
    has Yangtze on both sides
        so I can expect to eat delicious fish

and I can already smell
    fresh bamboo shoots
        growing on the mountain.

Here in my exile
    I'm not in charge
        just second in command

not the first or last poet
    to fill a minor post
        at the water works

but I feel myself unworthy
    given my low position
        and lack of accomplishments

still costing the regime
    an office and a salary
        and grain for making wine.

50. 正月二十日，往岐亭，郡人潘、古、郭、三人送余於女王城東禪莊院

十日春寒不出門

不知江柳已搖村

稍聞決決流冰谷

盡放青青沒燒痕

數畝荒園留我住

半瓶濁酒待君溫

去年今日關山路

細雨梅花正斷魂

50. On my way to Qiting

Chilly spring air
  for ten days
    I haven't stepped out of the house

and so I didn't notice
  how the willows have turned green
    stroking the whole village

or hear the faint sound
  of water laced with chunks of ice
    pouring into the valley

or gaze at the lush green grass
  newly growing
    where they burned last year's stubble.

I own a few acres
  barren field and garden
    thanks to friends

half a bottle of cloudy wine
  warmed up and waiting
    in case they come to visit.

This day one year ago
  I walked a long way
    through mountain roads and passes

the plum blossoms
  shining in the drizzle
    nearly broke my heart.

51. 東坡八首并敘
(其一)

廢壘無人顧

頹垣滿蓬蒿

誰能捐筋力

歲晚不償勞

獨有孤旅人

天窮無所逃

端來拾瓦礫

歲旱土不膏

崎嶇草棘中

欲刮一寸毛

51. The Eastern Slope (1st of 8)

A derelict campsite
   no one tending it

one ruined wall
   covered with wild grasses

who'd waste his strength
   working this land

when the results
   would never repay the labor?

But here I am, a solitary
   disregarded traveler

worn out under heaven
   nowhere else to turn

making an effort
   picking up tile shards

in a drought year
   soil not fertile

on this rugged patch
   thick grass, thorns and brambles

trying to scratch each inch
   clear of brush and weeds

喟焉釋未嘆
我廩何時高

I sigh and stop my plowing
    turning to ask

when will my granary fill
    and help me feed my family?

52. 正月二十日，與潘、郭二生出郊尋春，忽記去年是日同至女王城作詩，乃和前韻

東風未肯入東門

走馬還尋去歲春

人似秋鴻來有信

事如春夢了無痕

江城白酒三杯釅

野老蒼顏一笑溫

已約年年為此會

故人不用賦《招魂》

52. Spring saunter

The east winds aren't yet ready
    to blow through the eastern gate

we pass on horseback, seeking
    last year's springtime memory

we humans are like wild geese
    carrying messages in autumn

while the world's affairs, like dreams of spring,
    vanish and leave no trace.

Let's drink three cups
    of my good river-town wine

old rustics, hoary with years,
    quick with a warm smile.

We've already promised to meet
    here at this time each year

fast friends already, with no need
    to write sad songs or elegies.

53. 寒食雨二首
（其一）

自我來黃州
已過三寒食
年年欲惜春
春去不容惜
今年又苦雨
兩月秋蕭瑟
臥聞海棠花
泥污燕脂雪
暗中偷負去
夜半真有力

53. Rain and the Cold Food Festival (1st of 2)

Ever since
    I came to Huangzhou

we've had this festival
    three times.

Each year I've tried
    to fall in love with spring

it came and went
    and never returned my affection.

This year again
    we're suffering rain

two months more like
    a bleak and chilly autumn.

I lie here listening
    as cherry-apple blossoms fall

flower petals mixed with mud
    scattered on soft ground.

The season's disappearing
    secretly in the dark

kidnapped by force of rain
    at midnight

何殊病少年
病起頭已白

or like a young man
    overcome by illness

who wakes, recovering,
    to find his hair turned white!

54. 海棠

東風嫋嫋泛崇光
香霧空濛月轉廊
只恐夜深花睡去
故燒高燭照紅妝

54. Chinese flowering cherry-apple

A delicate east wind is blowing
    and there's a slender moon
        glowing overhead –

the night is fragrant, hazy,
    and the moon circles late
        above this dim pavilion.

I grow alarmed, this late,
    that the sleeping blooms are lonely
        and feel ignored

so I'm burning a group of candles
    expensive ones
        to light the lovely flowers.

55. 初入廬山三首
（其三）

芒鞋青竹杖

自挂百錢游

可怪深山裏

人人識故侯

55. First time into Lu Mountain (3rd of 3)

Wearing straw sandals
    holding a bamboo staff

adorned with copper coins
    roaming freely

how strange to go
    deep into this mountain

lots of people knew me
    aging bureaucrat.

56. 題西林壁

橫看成嶺側成峰
遠近高低總不同
不識廬山真面目
只緣身在此山中

56. Inscription for the wall at Westwood Temple near Lu Mountain

Looked at straight on
   it's a mountain ridge,
      viewed sideways, it's one peak –

close up, far off,
   high up or low down,
      it's never the same thing,

I'll never be able to see
   all the true features
      of this Lu Mountain

because I'm too close,
   smack in the middle
      of this big picture.

57. 邵伯梵行寺山茶

山茶相對阿誰栽

細雨無人我獨來

說似與君君不會

爛紅如火雪中開

57. Japanese camellias at Fanxing Temple

Two camellia trees
   facing each other
      wonder who planted them?

I've come by myself
   to visit them
      in this fine drizzle

I wanted to talk with them
   but that won't happen
      they are beyond language

brilliantly, thoroughly red,
   as if on fire
      blooming here in snow.

58. 漁父四首（其二）

漁父醉

蓑衣舞

醉裏却尋歸路

輕舟短櫂任橫斜

醒後不知何處

58. The fisherman (2nd of 4)

The fisherman
　　profoundly drunk

dancing around
　　in his palm-bark rain cape

drunk and searching for a way
　　to get back home

his little boat and oars
　　bobbing on the river

and when he sobers up
　　he won't remember where he was.

59. 書皇親畫扇

十年江海寄浮沈
夢繞江南黃葦林
誰謂風流貴公子
筆端還有五湖心

59. Poem on a fan painting

Ten years traveling
    on this country's lakes and rivers
        bobbing on the water

Dreams surround the delta
    you see reed marshes
        turning yellow everywhere

Who can blame young men of talent
    who love to party
        for their dissipation?

On the tip of every ink brush
    they still show concern
        for the welfare of this nation.

60. 和子由除夜元日省宿致齋三首（其三）

當年踏月走東風

坐看春闈鎖醉翁

白髮門生幾人在

却將新句調兒童

60. To my brother, at the New Year (3rd of 3)

Remember years ago
    walking in the moonlight
        wandering in east winds?

We'd sit around and watch
    the examination hall in spring
        one drunk old man inside …

White-haired disciples
    how many of us
        survive nowadays?

Still we bring
    new phrases
        hoping to teach them to children.

61. 王晉卿所藏著色山二首（其一）

縹緲營丘水墨仙

浮空出沒有無間

邇來一變風流盡

誰見將軍著色山

61. On a landscape painting (1st of 2)

It's misty and impressionistic
    this ink-brush painting
        in Li Cheng's celestial style

things float
    appear and disappear
        accidentally or by design

up to now
    the unconventional lifestyle
        seemed exhausted

because we hadn't seen this scroll
    belonging to the general
        who got to marry a princess.

62. 同秦仲二子雨中遊寶山

平明已報百吏散

半日來陪二子閑

立鵲低昂煙雨裏

行人出沒樹林間

62. At Spirit Mountain, touring with friends in rain

Daybreak and they say
    all bureaucrats
        should be off duty

and so I've spent the day
    strolling around
        with my two friends

here in the rain and mist
    big magpies soar
        rising up and diving down

while travelers cross
    appearing and disappearing
        among the groves of trees.

63. 與莫同年雨中飲湖上

到處相逢是偶然
夢中相對各華顛
還來一醉西湖雨
不見跳珠十五年

63. Savoring wine, on the lake, in the rain

It's the same thing everywhere
    encountering friends
        is mostly a matter of chance

in our dream
    we're suddenly face to face
        both of us white-haired!

Back on West Lake once again
    here in the rain
        falling-down drunk

haven't seen raindrops
    the size of jumping beads
        for fifteen years!

64. 次韻王忠玉游虎丘絕句三首（其二）

青蓋紅旗映玉山
新詩小草落玄泉
風流使者人爭看
知有真娘立道邊

64. Sightseeing at Tiger Hill (2nd of 3)

Blue umbrellas and red banners
    reflections of the legend of the Hill
        precious and noble as jade

newly written poems
    manuscripts cascading
        like the hanging springs of waterfalls

such an emissary, high-spirited,
    makes people want
        to stay around and watch

understanding that
    a gorgeous hostess
        will stand beside the road.

IV

1090–1101

65. 仲天貺、王元直自
眉山來見余錢塘，留半
歲，既行，作絕句五首
送之（其三）

三人一旦同行

留下高齋月明

遙想扁舟京口

尚餘孤枕潮聲

65. Saying goodbye to two visitors (3rd of 5)

One single day
    and the three young fellows
        gathered together

remembering the studio
    and how honorably they studied together
        in brilliant moonlight

remembering many years earlier
    passing the banks of the Yangtze
        in a little skiff

what I have left
    as I sleep alone
        is the sound of lapping waves.

66. 壽星院寒碧軒

清風肅肅搖窗扉
窗前修竹一尺圍
紛紛蒼雪落夏簟
冉冉綠霧沾人衣
日高山蟬抱葉響
人靜翠羽穿林飛
道人絕粒對寒碧
爲問鶴骨何緣肥

66. At the pavilion in the compound

A clear breeze
    blowing softly
        sways the window frames

beyond the window
    tall and straight bamboo
        growing thickly

thick and hazy snow
    falls heavily
        on summer mats

bit by bit
    fresh mist
        soaks our clothes

but the sun is rising high
    and mountain cicadas
        buzz on the tree trunks

the world is quiet
    as the blue kingfisher
        soars through the forest

as for the fasting virtue-seeker
    facing the forest
        the clear green groves

if he's really seeking virtue
    how did he grow
        so round and plump?

67. 又和景文韻

牡丹松檜一時栽
付與春風自在開
試問壁間題字客
幾人不爲看花來

67. To match a poem by a friend

Peony, pine, and cypress
    all were planted
        the same spring season

given the chance
    to face the spring winds openly
        carefree and at leisure

but ask those visitors
    who are writing their poems
        on the walls

how many of them came
    just to admire the flowers
        and neglect the evergreens.

68. 絕句

春來濯濯江邊柳
秋後離離湖上花
不羨千金買歌舞
一篇珠玉是生涯

68. Another quatrain

When spring has just arrived
    and willows by the river
        are glittering and sleek

or else when autumn comes
    luxurious, abundant,
        spreading flowers on the lake

I won't envy rich men
    who spend great sums of gold
        on troupes of entertainers

since even a poem's fragment
    precious as any jewel
        will furnish me with high life.

69. 贈劉景文

荷盡已無擎雨蓋
菊殘猶有傲霜枝
一年好景君須記
最是橙黃橘綠時

69. Poem for Liu

Summer's end, and the lotus
    no longer has big leaves
        that cradle raindrops

chrysanthemums have withered
    just a few branches left
        resisting frost

but you should keep in mind,
    old friend
        the year's best time –

it's early winter
    oranges ripening, tangerines greening,
        like your old age.

70. 再和楊公濟梅花十絕（其八）

湖面初驚片片飛

樽前吹折最繁枝

何人會得春風意

怕見梅黃雨細時

70. Rhymed to match Yang's plum poem (8th of 10)

On the lake's surface
   I'm startled to see
      flower flakes dancing

in front of my wine cup
   the wind scatters petals
      from plentiful branches

anyone who can sense
   the intentions
      behind spring breeze

will worry about the drizzle
   that will surely come
      at the time of the summer solstice.

71. 又書王晉卿畫四首
• 西塞風雨（其四）

斜風細雨到來時

我本無家何處歸

仰看雲天真箬笠

旋收江海入蓑衣

71. Poem on Wang's paintings (4th of 4)

When the wind blowing sideways
    combined with fine rain
        finally arrived

I had no place
    I could call home –
        where would I go?

I raise my head
    stare at the sky and the clouds
        like a conical bamboo hat

and imagine the rivers and seas
    circling and spinning
        are drenching my leafy raincloak.

72. 淮上早發

澹月傾雲曉角哀
小風吹水碧鱗開
此生定向江湖老
默數淮中十往來

72. Early morning departure, Huai River

A pure, pale moon, light clouds,
    the bugle's wake-up call
        sounds sad

a soft breeze
    ripples the water
        making small green waves

my life is pretty much settled
    aging at a distance
        from the circles of power

and I count quietly:
    it's ten times now
        I've had to cross this river.

73. 和陶飲酒二十首并敍 (其十五)

去鄉三十年

風雨荒舊宅

惟存一束書

寄食無定迹

每用愧淵明

尚取禾三百

頎然六男子

粗可傳清白

於吾豈不多

何事復歎息

73. Reading Tao Yuanming on 'Drinking Wine' (15th of 20)

Gone from my own home town
    some thirty years now

our old home
    probably weathered and desolate

all that's left
    a bundle of old letters

someone else would have to put me up
    no traces of my family

that's why I often think
    of Tao Yuanming

who managed to produce
    hundreds of classic poems ...

Well, there are six fine young men
    presently in this family

they can preserve and pass on
    our family's good name

that should content me
    don't you think?

why should I want to
    go around sighing?

74. 予少年頗知種松，
手植數萬株，皆中梁柱
矣。都梁山中見杜輿秀
才，求學其法，戲贈二
首（其一）

露宿泥行草棘中

十年春雨養髯龍

如今尺五城南杜

欲問東坡學種松

74. Planting pines with Du Yu (1st of 2)

Sleeping in open fields
    walking the muddy roads
        among the wilderness of thorn bushes

for ten years, in spring rains,
    I've been cultivating twisted pines
        into the shapes of dragons

turns out a member
    of the prestigious clan
        of the Du family

wants to ask me, Dongpo,
    advice on the methods
        of growing pine trees!

75. 上元侍飲樓上三首呈同列（其一）

澹月疎星遶建章

仙風吹下御爐香

侍臣鵠立通明殿

一朵紅雲捧玉皇

75. Imperial wine party (1st of 3)

Tranquil moonlight
    scattered stars
        around the Imperial Palace

enchanted breezes
    disperse the fragrance
        from the incense burner

here officials-in-waiting
    stood at attention
        in the Jade Emperor's courtyard

while the Emperor himself
    sat covered and concealed
        within a large red cloud.

76. 東府雨中別子由

庭下梧桐樹

三年三見汝

前年適汝陰

見汝鳴秋雨

去年秋雨時

我自廣陵歸

今年中山去

白首歸無期

客去莫歎息

主人亦是客

76. Parting from my brother in the rain

The parasol tree
still stands in the courtyard

I've seen you just three times
in the last three years

two years back
I traveled to Ruyin

saw you in autumn
in the sound of falling rain

and last year
also in the rainy season

I came back
from Guangling

this year they sent me
to Zhongshan

my hair is turning white
I fear I won't be back

I've been your guest and I'm leaving
no need for you to sigh

you've been the host
and you'll be a guest as well

對床定悠悠
夜雨空蕭瑟
起折梧桐枝
贈汝千里行
歸來知健否
莫忘此時情

the night drags by, we sit
face to face in the bedroom

the night rain sighs
rustling in desolate air

I break off a twig
from the parasol tree

give it to you, a memento
for your thousand mile journey

who knows if my health
will last till next time?

Let's promise not to forget
the way we feel right now!

77. 予前後守、倅餘杭，凡五年。夏秋之間，蒸熱不可過。獨中和堂東南頰，下瞰海門，洞視萬里，三伏常蕭然也。紹聖元年六月，舟行赴嶺外，熱甚。忽憶此處，而作是詩

忠孝王家千柱宮

東坡作吏五年中

中和堂上東南頰

獨有人間萬里風

77. Prompted by a memory

I recall the magnificent
    thousand-pillar palace
        of the royal household

I myself worked there
    as a petty official
        for five years

at the southeastern corner
    in the Hall of the Golden Mean
        overlooking the water

I could escape the heat
    and catch a fresh breeze
        to cheer our human world.

78. 和陶停雲四首并引
（其一）

停雲在空

黯其將雨

嗟我懷人

道修且阻

眷此區區

俯仰再撫

良辰過鳥

逝不我佇

78. Rhyming with Tao Yuanming (1st of 4)

Motionless clouds
  overhead

black sky
  about to rain

alas, I miss
  family and friends

the roads are long and rugged
  it's difficult to travel

an ordinary humbled man,
  I suffer from nostalgia

I bow my head, then lift it
  a simple gesture

on a brighter day
  there would be flocks of birds

time would pass more quickly
  I wouldn't be a statue.

79. 十二月十七日夜坐達曉，寄子由

燈燼不挑垂暗蕊

爐灰重撥尚餘薰

清風欲發鴉翻樹

缺月初升犬吠雲

閉眼此心新活計

隨身孤影舊知聞

雷州別駕應危坐

跨海清光與子分

79. Thinking about my brother

The lamp drops cinders
    the darkening candle wick
        hangs down

I poke the ashes in the stove
    over and over
        sniffing the last fragrance

a fresh breeze comes
    a crow flies up among the trees
        soaring and wheeling

the waning moon begins to rise
    dogs bark
        clouds pass

I close my eyes
    I feel my heart
        I need to plan my life

I'm traipsing after
    my own shadow
        longing for my oldest friend

while he, the magistrate
    may be sitting up too
        anxious, longing for me

across the sea between us
    the moon shines clear as crystal
        I share it with him now.

80. 過子忽出新意，以山芋作玉糝羹，色香味皆奇絕。天上酥陀則不可知，人間決無此味也

香似龍涎仍釅白

味如牛乳更全清

莫將南海金虀膾

輕比東坡玉糝羹

80. A favorite dish, my son's creation

The fragrant aroma
    is like dragon saliva
        rich and strong

the taste's as good
    as fresh cow milk
        yet purer, clearer,

don't even mention
    the famous leek and perch soup
        of the South Sea

it can't compare
    to Su Dongpo's
        sweet potato gruel!

81. 倦夜

倦枕厭長夜
小窗終未明
孤村一犬吠
殘月幾人行
衰鬢久已白
旅懷空自清
荒園有絡緯
虛織竟何成

81. A weary night

Tired, sleepless on my pillow
    worried all night long

the windows are still dark
    no sign of dawn

in this lonely village
    one dog barks all night

the moon wanes
    few people on the roads

my thinning hair
    has turned bright white

my years of travel have taught me
    how to be homesick

out in the empty fields
    spinster cicadas are buzzing

nothing to show for their labor
    nothing accomplished.

82. 次韻子由贈吳子野先生二絕句（其二）

江令蒼苔圍故宅

謝家語燕集華堂

先生笑說江南事

只有青山繞建康

82. Rhyming with Ziyou, for our friend Wu (2nd of 2)

The Magistrate's old home
    surrounded by weeds
        and dark green moss

the Xie clan's glorious mansion
    where gather flocks
        of twittering swallows –

my Lord, you entertained us
    with old tales, stories
        about the Yangtze Delta

here in Jiankang
    the capital city, circled
        by all these fresh green mountains.

83. 雨夜宿淨行院

芒鞋不踏利名場
一葉輕舟寄淼茫
林下對牀聽夜雨
靜無燈火照凄涼

83. Seeking lodging on a rainy night at Pure Life Monastery

Wearing straw sandals
   I've walked away
      from any wealth or fame

I'm like a little boat
   sensing an expanse
      of endless water

here under groves of trees
   face to face in the bedroom
      listening all night to the rain

silence, no lamplight
   only a deep sense
      of pity and desolation.

84. 贈嶺上梅

梅花開盡百花開

過盡行人君不來

不趁青梅嘗煮酒

要看細雨熟黃梅

84. Flowering plums among mountains

The plums are in full bloom
    thousands of flowers
        opening everywhere

people arrive and leave
    so many passersby
        but you, dear sir, aren't here

why not come visit me
    among these blossoming plums –
        I'll warm up some wine

we can watch the plums
    turning ripe and golden
        here in fine drizzling rain.

85. 次韻法芝舉舊詩一首

春來何處不歸鴻

非復羸牛踏舊踪

但願老師心似月

誰家甕裏不相逢

85. Rhymed with Fazhi, after an old poem

Spring's here –
    where can you not find
        swans and geese returning?

I no longer feel thin and weak
    a frail ox trampling
        along old trails and traces

I'm hoping you can remain
    the poet-priest you are
        heart-pure and bright, a full moon,

and maybe you'll encounter me
    in someone's earthenware water jar
        clear in your own reflection.

V

POEMS OF UNCERTAIN DATE

86. 附江南本織錦圖上回文原作三首（其一）

春晚落花餘碧草

夜涼低月半枯桐

人隨野雁邊城暮

雨映疎簾繡閣空

86. Palindrome style (1st of 3)

Late spring
    most blossoms fallen
        sparing some dark green grass

cooling at night
    moonrise low
        Tung trees withered, yellow

people following wild geese
    frontier forts and towns
        face deepening dusk

raindrops on screen shades
    the decorated parlor
        sits empty.

87. 洗兒戲作

人皆養子望聰明
我被聰明誤一生
惟願孩兒愚且魯
無災無難到公卿

87. Baby's first bath

Parents raising children
    hope they will become
        intelligent and wise

but all my life
    I've been the victim
        of my own cleverness

all I want for my kids
    is that they be
        ignorant and stupid

so they can grow into
    high-ranking nobles
        free from misfortunes and suffering.

88. 夢中絕句

楸樹高花欲插天
暖風遲日共茫然
落英滿地君方見
惆悵春光又一年

88. In my dream

Manchurian catalpas grow
    tall and flowering
        sticking up into the sky

genial breezes
    blowing warm in springtime
        leave us looking blank

fallen blossoms
    spread around on the ground
        just observe it, sir!

Another year gone by
    leaving me disconsolate
        touched in my heart.

89. 春夜

春宵一刻值千金
花有清香月有陰
歌管樓臺聲細細
鞦韆院落夜沉沉

214

89. Spring night pleasures

One short moment
    of sensual spring night –
        worth more than a thousand gold coins

the flowers' lucid fragrance
    moonlight making shadows
        hinting pleasure

distant sounds of singing
    flutes and strings
        drifting from the theater

and here in the playground
    rope swings hang
        deep in the stillness of night.

90. 水月寺

千尺長松掛薜蘿
梯雲嶺上一聲歌
湖山深秀有何處
水月池中桂影多

90. Moon-Water Temple

Thousand-foot pines
    towering overhead
        full of climbing figs and lichens

high on the cloud-ladder mountain
    I overheard
        a loud voice singing

vast mountain ranges
    deep faraway lakes –
        what does it matter?

here is the moon on the water
    of this full pond
        casting shadows.

91. 戲答佛印

遠公沽酒飲陶潛
佛印燒豬待子瞻
採得百花成蜜後
不知辛苦為誰甜

91. Teasing the priest

The priest Huiyuan, they say,
    purchased wine at the wine-shop
        for the poet Tao Yuanming

now my friend, Priest Foyin,
    has roasted a whole pig
        to entertain yours truly

all the work of finding flowers
    gathering nectar
        turning out honey

lots of toil and hardship
    and who is it for
        that sweetness?

92. 失題三首（其二）

望斷水雲千里

橫空一抹晴嵐

不見邯鄲歸路

夢中略到江南

92. Title lost (2nd of 3)

Gazing a thousand miles
    landscape of water and clouds

horizontal sky
    a stripe of misty light

I don't see any return
    back to my old hometown

it's only in my dreams
    I visit the Yangtze Delta.

93. 轆轤歌

新繫青絲百尺繩
心在君家轆轤上
我心皎潔君不知
轆轤一轉一惆悵
何處春風吹曉幕
江南綠水通珠閣
美人二八顏如花
泣向花前畏花落
臨春風
聽春鳥
別時多
見時少

93. Song of the windlass

I've tied up my black hair
    with a hundred feet of rope

as I work at the windlass my heart
    is with my husband's family

my heart's so pure, my dear,
    you'd hardly recognize it

every turn of the windlass
    adds to my sadness

spring breezes come from nowhere
    blowing the curtains each morning

in the Delta region blue-green water
    slides past elegant pavilions

beautiful young teens
    with fresh and flowery faces

weep tears beside the blooming shrubs
    afraid for the shedding petals

spring breezes blowing

hearing songbirds singing

longer separations

shorter times together

愁人一夜不得眠
瑶井玉繩相對曉

all night long this anxious person
    could not fall asleep

watching two constellations
    facing each other till dawn.

94. 秋日寄友人

柳條風煖會吟時
林下池邊屐齒移
別後過從更疎懶
暮蟬嘹亂不勝悲

94. Sent to a friend on an autumn day

(attribution questioned)

Slender willow wands
    warm and genial breezes
        a time to gather and write poems

under the groves of trees
    beside the brimming ponds
        footsteps of friends on the move

since we last said goodbye
    I've grown more idle and lazy
        about meeting or staying in touch

sunset and the cicadas
    set up a ragged chorus
        enlarging my sadness.

95. 山村二首（其一）

野水開冰出
山雲帶雨行
白鷗乘曉泛
黃犢試春耕
地僻民風古
年豐米價平
村居自瀟灑
況有讀書聲

95. Mountain Village (1st of 2)

An icy field in open country
    thawing out and flowing

mountain clouds and rain
    blowing past in showers

white gulls out before dawn
    gliding and drifting

yellow calves, yoked together
    for the spring ploughing

this place is so out-of-the-way
    its customs are antiquated

but this is a harvest year
    and the price of grain is stable

village life can be tranquil
    natural and unrestrained

plus there's the pleasant sound
    of children at their lessons.

96. 詩四句

岡陵來勢遠
幽處更依山
一片湖景內
千家市井間

96. Fragments

From this high mound
    one can see a great distance

while this secluded spot
    feels closer to the mountains

here among layers
    of lake-view scenery

and countless households
    market towns, people, shops.

NOTES

Our work on Su Shi (also known by his sobriquet Su Dongpo, or simply Dongpo) is based on the edition of *Su Shi shiji* (蘇軾詩集), published by Beijing Zhonghua shuju (北京中華書局), 1982 (1987 printing), 8-volume set.

With regard to Chinese characters and Romanization, we consistently use traditional Chinese characters (傳統漢字) and the Chinese Hanyu Pinyin system (漢語拼音).

1. "Watching the moon after coming by boat to Niukou Island"

- Written in 1059
- 26 lines, 5 characters per line
- Title in Chinese: Niukou jian yue

1. Niukou 牛口, in Xingyang County 滎陽縣, present-day Henan Province.
2. Bingshen nian 丙申年, the year Bingshen, i.e. 1056, "three years ago."
3. The capital, Northern Song dynasty's (960-1127) capital city Bianjing 汴京 is modern Kaifeng 開封, present-day Henan Province.
4. Longjin Bridge 龍津橋, a business district inside the capital city.

2. "Looking up at mountains from the river"

- Written in 1059
- 8 lines, 7 characters per line
- Title in Chinese: Jiang shang kan shan

  1. While the poet was sailing along the Yangtze River through Jingzhou 荊州 area, in present-day Hubei Province.

3. "The Waiting-for-Husband Terrace"

- Written in 1059
- 8 lines, 7 characters per line
- Title in Chinese: Wangfutai

  1. Waiting-for-Husband Terrace, Wangfutai 望夫臺, nearby Zhongzhou 忠州 on the bank of the Yangtze River (in present-day Sichuan Province, now within Chongqing City). It was a place associated in the local folklore about a wife, whose husband had left home a long time before, standing on this terrace that overlooked the river as she waited for him to return.

4. "At Princess Zhaojun's village"

- Written in 1059
- 10 lines: 6 lines of 5 characters and 4 lines of 7 characters
- Title in Chinese: Zhaojuncun

  1. Wang Zhaojun 王昭君, born ca. 51-15 BCE in ancient

State of Chu 楚, now Hubei Province; one of the four beauties of ancient China. An imperial concubine of the Han court (in the Western Han dynasty, 206 BCE-23 AD), she was sent by the Han emperor to marry to the king of the neighboring Xiongnu 匈奴 empire.

2. Menmei 門楣, lintel of a door, referring to family status.

5. "Poem in reply to my brother's poem of nostalgia for Mianchi"

- Written in 1061
- 8 lines, 7 characters per line
- Title in Chinese: He Ziyou Mianchi huaijiu

1. This is one of Su Dongpo's best-known poems.
2. Ziyou 子由, Su Dongpo's younger brother Su Zhe 蘇轍 (1039-1112) using his courtesy name Ziyou.
3. Mianchi 澠池: Mianchi County, west of Luoyang city, in present-day Henan Province.

Poem 6. "The willow tree"

- Written in 1062
- 4 lines, 5 characters per line
- Title in Chinese: Liu (tree)

1. As a part of "次韻子由岐下詩并引" (Ci yun Ziyou Qi xia shi bing yin). One of 21 poems expressing fondness for tree planting that Su Dongpo composed in the same rhyme to his brother Ziyou.

7. "Inscribed on a fancy pavilion in Shaanxi"

- Written in 1062
- 8 lines, 7 characters per line
- Title in Chinese: Ti Baojixian Sifeige

1. Sifeige 斯飛閣, a pavilion of luxurious, colorful structure in Baoji 寶雞 County (in present-day Shaanxi 陝西 Province).

8. "At the Celestial Harmony Temple in Shaanxi"

- Written in 1063
- 8 lines, 5 characters per line
- Title in Chinese: Fufeng Tianhesi

1. Tianhesi 天和寺 (Celestial Harmony Temple), in Fufeng 扶風 (in present-day Shaanxi (陝西)Province).

9. "Green Bamboo Pavilion"

- Written in 1070
- 8 lines, 5 characters per line
- Title in Chinese: Lüyunting

1. Lüyunting 綠筠亭, a pavilion/kiosk named "green bamboo skin."
2. Tao Jingjie 陶靖節, i.e. Tao Qian 陶潛, aka Tao Yuanming 陶淵明, 365-427, the renowned "recluse poet" of the "fields and gardens" (tianyuan 田園) poetry genre.

10. "Response to a poem found in a boat"

- Written in 1071
- 4 lines, 5 characters per line
- Title in Chinese: Chu du lai Chen, suo cheng chuanshang you ti xiaoshi ba shou, bu zhi heren you gan yu yu xin zhe, liao wei he zhi (qi san)

  1. Chinese title "Chu du lai Chen …" indicates: departing from capital city on the way to his new assignment in Hangzhou (in present-day Zhejiang Province), and passing through Chenzhou 陳州 Prefecture (in present-day Henan Province).

11. "Traveling between provinces"

- Written in 1071
- 8 lines, 7 characters per line
- Title in Chinese: Chu Yingkou chu jian Huaishan, shiri zhi Shouzhou

  1. Yingkou 潁口, in Yingshang County 潁上縣 (in present-day Anhui Province), which the Huaihe 淮河 River flows through.
  2. Shouzhou 壽州, modern Shouxian 壽縣 (in present-day Anhui Province).

12. "Visiting two monks on a winter day"

- Written in 1071
- 21 lines: first 2 lines, 3 characters per line; plus 19 lines, 7

characters per line
- Title in Chinese: Lari you Gushan fang Huiqin Huisi er seng

1. Lari 臘日, the day of winter sacrifice (3 days after the solstice, about December 25).
2. Gushan 孤山 (Lonely Mountain), in West Lake 西湖 (Xi Hu), Hangzhou.
3. Huiqin 惠勤 and Huisi 惠思, two poet-monks/Daoist priests.
4. Baoyunshan 寶雲山 (Treasure Cloud Mountain).

13. "At a temple, asked to help name a pavilion"

- Written in 1072
- 4 lines, 7 characters per line
- Title in Chinese: Jixiangsi seng qiu ge ming

1. Jixiangsi 吉祥寺 (Auspiciousness Temple).
2. "Se" 色 (reality), "kong" 空 (nihility). Here Su Dongpo is referring to the Buddhist "Heart Sutra" (心經 *Xinjing*).

14. "At a temple in the mountains, during rain"

- Written in 1072
- 5 lines: first 2 lines, 3 characters per line; plus 3 lines, 7-character per line
- Title in Chinese: Yuzhong you Tianzhu Linggan Guanyinyuan

1. Tianzhu(shan) 天竺山 (Mount Tianzhu), in Hangzhou.

2. Linggan Guanyinyuan 靈感觀音院 (Inspirational Bodhisattva Guanyin Temple).

3. The white-robed Goddess of Mercy referring to 白衣仙人 (Baiyi xianren), i.e. Guanyin 觀音.

15. "Floating at night on West Lake (2nd of 5)"

- Written in 1072
- 4 lines, 7 characters per line
- Title in Chinese: Ye fan Xihu wu jue (qi er)

1. West Lake 西湖 (Xi Hu), a very popular sightseeing attraction in Hangzhou.

2. "Jue" i.e. "jueju" 絕句 (Chinese quatrain).

16. "Night view at Ocean-Gazing Pavilion (4th of 5)"

- Written in 1072
- 4 lines, 7 characters per line
- Title in Chinese: Wanghai Lou wanjing wu jue (qi si)

1. Wanghailou 望海樓 (Ocean-Gazing Pavilion), in Hangzhou.

17. "Written to match a Chan (Zen) priest's poem"

- Written in 1072
- 6 lines, 5 characters per line
- Title in Chinese: Fantiansi jian seng Shouquan xiao shi qingwan keai, ci yun

1. Fantiansi 梵天寺 (Temple of Heavenly Mansions), in Hangzhou.
2. Shouquan 守詮, a Chan (Zen) poet-priest.

18. "Enjoying the lanterns at Lucky Charm Temple"

- Written in 1073
- 8 lines, 7 characters per line
- Title in Chinese: Xiangfusi Jiuqu guan deng

1. Xiangfusi 祥符寺, (Lucky Charm Temple), in Hangzhou.
2. Jiuqu 九曲, a neighborhood of Hangzhou.

19. "Drinking on West Lake, clear first, then rain (2nd of 2)"

- Written in 1073
- 4 lines, 7 characters per line
- Title in Chinese: Yin hushang chu qing hou yu er shou (qi er)

1. This is one of Su Dongpo's best-known poems. The first two lines (水光潋灩 Shuiguang lianyan ..., 山色空濛 Shanse kongmeng ...) are highly praised as stunningly beautiful.
2. Xizi 西子, i.e. Xi Shi 西施, b. 506 B.C., one of the four great beauties of ancient China.
3. West Lake 西湖 (Xi Hu), in Hangzhou, present-day Zhejiang Province.

20. "On the road to Xincheng (1st of 2)"

- Written in 1073
- 8 lines, 7 characters per line
- Title in Chinese: Xincheng dao zhong er shou (qi yi)

1. Xincheng 新城, in present-day Zhejiang Province.

21. "In a mountain village (1st of 5)"

- Written in 1073
- 4 lines, 7 characters per line
- Title in Chinese: Shancun wu jue (qi yi)

22. "Encountering a monk near his temple"

- Written in 1073
- 10 lines: 7 lines, 5 characters per line; 1 line, 6 characters per line; plus 2 lines, 7 characters per line
- Title in Chinese: Yuqian seng Lüyunxuan

1. Yuqian 於潛: Yuqian County, nearby Hangzhou, in present-day Zhejiang Province.
2. Yuqian seng 於潛僧, a monk of Yuqian County, named Huijue 惠覺.
3. Lüyunxuan 綠筠軒, Green Bamboo Pavilion/Veranda. See also poem #9.
4. 此君, ci jun (this fellow), a nickname for bamboo in classical Chinese poetry.
5. 揚州鶴, Yangzhou he (Yangzhou crane). Legend goes that a Yangzhou crane will bring a person official rank, wealth,

and the gift of becoming an immortal, the three best wishes of life.

23. "Roadside flowers (1st of 3)"

- Written in 1073
- 4 lines, 7 characters per line
- Title in Chinese: Mo shang hua san shou (qi yi)

24. "The Double Ninth Festival, a visit by boat to two priests (2nd of 2)"

- Written in 1073
- 8 lines, 7 characters per line
- Title in Chinese: Jiuri, xun Zhen sheli, sui fan xiaozhou zhi Qinshiyuan, er shou (qi er)

1. 九日, Jiuri (Ninth day of the ninth month, i.e. Chongyang (Double Ninth) Festival.
2. 臻闍黎, Zhen sheli, Monk Zhen is referred to as a "sheli," which is an honorific term for high priest.
3. 勤師院, Qinshiyuan, Priest Qin's temple.
4. 白足赤髭, Baizu (Cleanfoot) and Chizi (Redbeard), two high priests.
5. 桑苧, Sangzhu (the old man Sangzhu, i.e. the "Sage of Tea" Lu 陸羽, 733-804).

25. "Written in praise of a monk's cell (1st of 2)"

- Written in 1073

242

- 4 lines, 7 characters per line
- Title in Chinese: Shu Shuangzhu Zhanshi fang er shou (qi yi)

1. Shuangzhu(si) 雙竹(寺) (Double Bamboo Temple), in Hangzhou.
2. Zhanshi 湛師 (Monk Zhanshi).

26. "Touring two temples (2nd of 2)"

- Written in 1074
- 8 lines, 5 characters per line
- Title in Chinese: You Helin, Zhaoyin er shou (qi er)

1. 鶴林、招隱, Helin (Crane Forest) and Zhaoyin (Inviting Reclusion) Temples.

27. "Sent to a friend (2nd of 5)"

- Written in 1074
- 8 lines, 7 characters per line
- Title in Chinese: Chang Run daozhong, you huai Qiantang, ji Shugu wu shou (qi er)

1. Chang Run 常潤, referring to Changzhou 常州 (in Jiangsu Province) and Runzhou 潤州 (present day Zhenjiang 鎮江, in Jiangsu Province).
2. Qiantang 錢塘, referring to Hangzhou 杭州.
3. Shugu 述古, i.e. Chen Xiang 陳襄 (1017-1080).
4. Jiangnan 江南, River South, i.e. the Yangtze Delta.
5. Xueyi 雪衣 (snow coat), referring to white-coated

pigeons.

28. "The temple on Black Ox Ridge"

- Written in 1074
- 9 lines: 7 lines, 7 characters per line; plus 2 lines, 5 characters per line
- Title in Chinese: Qingniuling gao jue chu, you xiaosi, jenji han dao

1. Qingniuling 青牛嶺 (Black Ox Ridge), in Xincheng 新城, present-day Zhejiang Province.

29. "Saying goodbye to a friend (1st of 2)"

- Written in 1075
- 8 lines, 5 characters per line
- Title in Chinese: Chucheng songke, buji, buzhi xishang, er shou (qi yi)

1. Shijun 使君 (This term may refer to a censor, governor, or gentry).

30. "Poem in answer to my brother (2nd of 4)"

- Written in 1075
- 8 lines, 7 characters per line
- Title in Chinese: He Ziyou si shou (qi er: Song chun)

1. Brother Ziyou referring to Su Dongpo's younger brother

Su Zhe. See also poem #5.

2. Buddhist mantra "Fajieguan 法界觀," a method of practice in the Huayan or Flower Garland school of Buddhism (華嚴宗 Huayanzong). It is based on the Avatamsaka Sutra (華嚴經 *Huayanjing*).

31. "My little child"

- Written in 1075
- 10 lines, 5 characters per line
- Title in Chinese: Xiaoer

1. "That wife of olden times," Liu Ling's 劉伶 wife (who would not permit her husband to have money for purchasing wine).
2. Liu Ling, 221-300, was a Chinese poet and scholar. One of the Seven Sages of the Bamboo Grove, Liu Ling was a Daoist. Popularly regarded as an eccentric, he was notorious for his love of alcohol. His wife refused to let him buy any more wine.

32. "A dream of my dead wife: To the tune, 'Of Jinling'"

- Written in 1075
- 16 long and short sentences, 3- or 4- or 7-character per sentence
- Title in Chinese: Jiangchengzi (yimao zhengyue ershiri ye ji meng)

1. Extra selection. "Ci" (詞) style poetry (with lines of irregular lengths) is a poetic form in the Song dynasty and

viewed as a different genre from traditional "shi" (詩) style poetry.

2. Su Dongpo wrote this piece of "ci" style poetry for his deceased first wife Lady Wang Fu 王弗(1039-1065), on the occasion of the 10th anniversary of her passing. Su (1037-1101) married Wang Fu in 1054, at age 17 and 15 respectively. They stayed happily married for 11 years. She died in 1065 at age 26. In 1075, Dongpo wrote this "ci" poem in loving memory of her. One of his best-known poems, it is very touching and sentimental.

3. Jiangchengzi (江城子): name of the tune of this "ci" poem, literally meaning: river/city wall/a small piece; the poem is also known in English as, To the tune, "Of Jinling" (Jinling is modern Nanjing).

4. The year "yimao" falls on 1075.

33. "Another poem for Wen Tong and his gardens (16th of 30)"

• Written in 1076
• 4 lines, 7 characters per line
• Title in Chinese: He Wen Yuke Yangchuan yuanchi sanshi shou: Luxiangting (qi shiliu)

1. Su Dongpo's friend Wen Yuke 文與可 (i.e. Wen Tong 文同, 1018-1079), maintained flower gardens in Yangchuan County 洋川郡 (in Yangzhou 洋州 Prefecture, modern Yang County 洋縣, present-day Shaanxi (陝西) Province).

2. Luxiangting 露香亭 (Fragrance of Morning Dew Pavilion), a structure in the gardens.

246

34. "Climbing Mount Chang to visit the temple"

- Written in 1076
- 20 lines, 5 characters per line
- Title in Chinese: Deng Changshan jueding Guangliting

1. Mount Chang 常山 (Changshan), in Mizhou 密州 (Modern Zhucheng 諸城, in present-day Shandong Province).
2. Guangliting 廣麗亭 (Broad Beauty Temple).
3. Mulingguan 穆陵關 (Majestic Mounds Pass), Langyatai 瑯邪臺 (Langyatai Terrace observation platform), Jiuxianshan 九仙山 (Mountain of Nine Immortals), some major landmarks viewed by the poet on top of the mountain.
4. Yu Shun 虞舜, i.e. Emperor Shun, a legendary (supposedly earlier than 2700 B.C.) ruler of ancient China, and one of the Three Sovereigns and Five Emperors.
5. Penglai 蓬萊 refers to an immortal realm that was believed to be a floating island in the ocean somewhere off the east coast of China

35. "Eulogy for Wang"

- Written in 1076
- 8 lines, 7 characters per line
- Title in Chinese: Tongnian Wang Zhongfu wanci

1. Wang Zhongfu 王中甫 (i.e. Wang Jie 王介, 1015-1087) was a colleague of Su Dongpo.
2. "The late Emperor" referring to Emperor Renzong of the

Song dynasty 宋仁宗, 1010-1063; reign 1022-1063.

3. Pengkun 鵬鵾 – The brilliant Daoist philosopher Zhuangzi (Chuang-tzu) 莊子, 369-286 B.C., using the term "pengkun" (big fabulous bird of enormous size) to refer to men of great talent and bold vision.

4. Jingkou 京口, modern Zhenjiang 鎮江, in present-day Jiangsu Province.

36. "Pear blossom poem for Kong (3rd of 5)"

- Written in 1077
- 4 lines, 7 characters per line
- Title in Chinese: He Kong Mizhou wu jue: Donglan lihua (qi san)

1. Kong Mizhou 孔密州, i.e. Kong Zonghan 孔宗翰, d. 1088, 46th generation descendent of Confucius.
2. Qingming(jie) 清明 Festival, around early April, also called Tomb-Sweeping Day.

37. "Sun Gate Pass (3rd of 3)"

- Written in 1077
- 4 lines, 7 characters per line
- Title in Chinese: Yangguan ci san shou: Zhongqiu yue (qi san)

1. Yangguan 陽關, or Yangguan Pass (literally: "Sun Gate"), is a mountain pass fortified by Emperor Wu (reigning 141-87 BCE) of the Western Han dynasty and was used for centuries as an outpost in ancient China. It is located

southwest of Dunhuang, in present-day Gansu Province. In ancient times, this territory was the westernmost administrative center of China. The term "Yangguan" is typically associated with parting, farewell, and longtime separation.
2. Zhongqiu 中秋, Mid-autumn Moon Festival, around mid-September to early October.
3. Yinhan 銀漢 (or Yinhe 銀河), denotes the Milky Way.
4. Yupan 玉盤, literally jade plate, refers to the moon.

38. "Qianzhou scenes (7th of 8)"

- Written in 1078
- 4 lines, 7 characters per line
- Title in Chinese: "Qianzhou ba jing tu" ba shou, bing yin (qi qi)

1. Qianzhou 虔州, modern Ganzhou 贛州, in present-day Jiangxi Province.
2. Yugutai 鬱孤臺 (Melancholy and Solitary Pavilion) is located in Ganzhou City, present-day Jiangxi Province.
3. Zhifu 之罘 or 芝罘, Zhifu Island (芝罘島 Zhifudao), is an islet in Shandong Province. The name of the islet Chefoo was generalized to mean the entire Yantai 烟台 region.
4. Haishi 海市, or Haishi shenlou 海市蜃樓, meaning mirage.
5. Jianggong 絳宮, meaning bright-red colored palaces.
6. Penglai 蓬萊; see also poem #34.

39. "For Zimei, on his being sick"

- Written in 1078
- 4 lines, 7 characters per line
- Title in Chinese: Guan Zimei bingzhong zuo, jietan bu zu, yin ci yun

1. Zimei 子美, real name Fu Guobo 傅國博, a friend of Su Dongpo.
2. Ci yun 次韻, using the rhyme sequence of a poem when replying to it.

40. "For Wang Gong, on the Double Ninth Festival"

- Written in 1078
- 8 lines, 7 characters per line
- Title in Chinese: Jiu ri ci yun Wang Gong

1. Jiuri 九日, Chongyang (Double Ninth) Festival. See also poem #24.
2. Ci yun 次韻, see also poem #39.
3. Wang Gong 王鞏, courtesy name Dingguo 定國, fl. 1068-1077; a good friend of Su Dongpo.
4. Congshi 從事, a minor bureaucracy position. Qingzhou 青州, a county in present-day Shandong Province. "Qingzhou congshi" as a term is an allusion referring to fine wine.
5. Sanqian zhang 三千丈, three thousand "Chinese feet" in measurement, implying very long.
6. Yibai chou 一百籌, hundred times/pieces of poems. Wang is known for writing a plenitude of poems quickly.
7. Dongge 東閣, east side chamber of a noble man or high

official's residence, used for receiving visitors.

8. Mingri huanghua 明日黃花, yellow chrysanthemum became useless the day after Chongyang Festival.

41. "Inscription for a landscape painting"

- Written in 1078
- 13 lines: 8 lines, 7 characters per line; 2 lines, 3 characters per line; plus 3 lines, 5 characters per line
- Title in Chinese: Li Sixun hua "Changjiang jue dao tu"

1. Li Sixun 李思訓, 651-716, a Tang dynasty artist and founder of what became known as the northern school of Chinese landscape painting.
2. Changjiang 長江, Yangtze River.
3. Dagushan 大孤山, in Poyang Lake 鄱陽湖, along the Yangtze River around Hukou County 湖口縣, in present-day Jiangxi Province.
4. Xiaogushan 小孤山, along the Yangtze River in Pengze County 彭澤縣, present-day Jiangxi Province. There is another Xiaogushan, also along the Yangtze River in Susong County 宿松縣, in present-day Anhui Province.
5. Xiaogu 小姑, meaning young sister or young lady, is a homonym of the Xiaogushan mountain 小孤山.
6. Penglang 彭郎, Gentleman Peng, is a homonym of Penglangji 澎浪磯, a rock facing Xiaogushan in the river. This is a reference to a local legend.

42. "Climbing Dragon-Cloud Mountain"

- Written in 1078

- 7 lines, 7 characters per line (Usually 8 lines, but this 7-line format is unusual)
- Title in Chinese: Deng Yunlongshan

1. Yunlongshan 雲龍山 (Dragon-Cloud Mountain) and Huangmaogang 黃茅岡 (Yellow Cogongrass Ridge), in Xuzhou 徐州 (present-day Jiangsu Province).
2. Shijun 使君, honorific title of a civil governor (Sir). See also poem #29.

43. "Moon viewing at the Yellow Tower"

- Written in 1078
- 8 lines, 7 characters per line
- Title in Chinese: Shiyue shiwu ri guan yue Huanglou, xi shang ci yun

1. Huanglou 黃樓 (literally yellow building), Yellow Tower, a multistoried, tall building in Xuzhou 徐州 (in present-day Jiangsu Province) constructed under Su Dongpo while serving as prefect (magistrate).
2. Ci yun 次韻, using the rhyme sequence to reply. See also poems #39, 40.
3. Zhongqiu 中秋, Mid-autumn Festival. See also poem #37.
4. Futu 浮圖, or 浮屠, Buddhist pagoda.
5. Sanxia 三峽 (the Three Gorges), three adjacent gorges along the middle reaches of the Yangtze River, in the hinterland of China.
6. Wuhu 五湖, a string of lakes along the lower Yangtze Delta.
7. Shijun 使君, referring to a magistrate. See also poem #42.

44. "Poem written on a snowy day"

- Written in 1078
- 8 lines, 5 characters per line
- Title in Chinese: He Tian Guobo xi xue

1. Tian Guobo 田國博, a friend and colleague of Su Dongpo.
2. Yuhua 玉花, snowflakes.
3. Cuilang 翠浪, seedlings of cereal crops.
4. Mingte 螟螣, snout-moth larvae.
5. Zhongqing 鐘磬, musical bells and musical stones (classical Chinese musical instruments).

45. "Drinking in moonlight by the apricot orchard"

- Written in 1079
- 12 lines, 7 characters per line
- Title in Chinese: Yueye yuke yin xinghua xia

1. While in Xuzhou 徐州 (in present-day Jiangsu Province), Su Dongpo entertained three of his guests. Two of the younger guests played bamboo flutes.
2. This is a typical Su Dongpo poem, connecting friends, moon, flowers, and wine.
3. Dongxiao 洞簫, vertical end-blown bamboo-flute.

46. "Missing my meeting with a priest"

- Written in 1079
- 4 lines, 5 characters per line

- Title in Chinese: Zhashang fang daoren bu yu

1. Zhashang 霅上, another name of Huzhou 湖州 (in Zhejiang Province).
2. Daoren 道人, Buddhist priest, referring to 参寥 Canliao, full name He Daoqian 何道潛, style name Canliao, gifted in literature and poetry, a good friend of Dongpo.
3. Qingyan 青眼: dark eyeballs, symbolizing positive attitude treating people with favor and good grace, compared to "bai yan 白眼"; white eyeballs, symbolizing negative attitude treating others with supercilious look. Thus, "qingyanren" (青眼人) means a gentle person with dark eyeballs.

47. "From prison, to my brother (1st of 2)"

- Written in 1079
- 8 lines, 7 characters per line
- Title in Chinese: Yu yi shi xi yushitai yu, yuli shao jian qin, zi du buneng kan, si yuzhong, bude yi bie Ziyou, gu he er shi shou yuzu Liang Cheng, yi wei Ziyou, er shou (qi yi)

1. A 42-character lengthy title. Alternative title in shorter 7-character is called: 獄中寄子由二首 = Yuzhong ji Ziyou er shou = From prison sending two poems to Brother Ziyou.
2. Yushitai 御史臺, the Censorate supervisory agency. This was the infamous "Crow Terrace (Censorate) Poetry Trial 烏臺詩案 (Wutai shian)" of 1079.
3. Brother Ziyou, i.e. Su Zhe (蘇轍, 1039-1112).
4. Bainian 百年, hundred years, meaning: after long long years, time of death.

5. Jun 君: a princely fellow, a person of noble character, a gentleman.
6. Laisheng 來生: next life. Su Dongpo chose this phrase to reveal his Buddhist concept of reincarnation.

48. "The plum trees (1st of 2)"

- Written in 1080
- 4 lines, 7 characters per line
- Title in Chinese: Meihua er shou (qi yi)

1. Su Dongpo wrote "The plum trees" during his journey to new demotion assignment in Huangzhou 黄州 (in present-day Hubei Province) as a result of his "Crow Terrace (Censorate) Poetry Trial of 1079."
2. Du guanshan 度關山 (Crossing the forts and hills), implying surviving the ordeals of the "Poetry Trial." Guanshan 關山 was also a place name in Macheng 麻城 (present-day Hubei Province).

49. "Arriving in Huangzhou for the first time"

- Written in 1080
- 8 lines, 7 characters per line
- Title in Chinese: Chu dao Huangzhou

1. Huangzhou 黄州, modern Huanggang 黄岡 City (in present-day Hubei Province).
2. Yuanwai 員外, second class officer.
3. Shuicaolang 水曹郎, petty officer at "Shuibusi" 水部司 (the department of water works) within "Gongbu" 工部

(the Ministry of Public Works).

4. Yajiunang 壓酒囊: literally a pocket (sack) of wine-making grains, part of official salary in kind.

50. "On my way to Qiting"

- Written in 1081
- 8 lines, 7 characters per line
- Title in Chinese: Zhengyue ershi ri, wang Qiting, junren Pan, Gu, Guo sanren song yu yu Nüwangcheng Dongchanzhuangyuan

1. Zhengyue ershi ri: the 20th day of the first month, this day was significant to Su Dongpo—the day in 1075 he dreamed of his late wife Wang Fu.
2. Qiting 岐亭, modern day Qiting Township, in Macheng 麻城 City (Hubei Province). Su was visiting there to see a good friend Chen Zao 陳慥 (or Chen Jichang 陳季常, fl. 11th cent.).
3. Pan, Gu, Guo (Pan Bing 潘丙, Gu Gengdao 古耕道, and Guo Gou 郭遘), three good friends of Su Dongpo.
4. Nüwangcheng 女王城 Castle (literally, female monarch castle).
5. Dongchanzhuangyuan 東禪莊院 (Dongchan (Eastern meditation) Hall).

51. "The Eastern Slope (1st of 8)"

- Written in 1081
- 12 lines, 5 characters per line
- Title in Chinese: Dongpo ba shou bingxu (qi yi)

1. Dong po 東坡 (Eastern Slope), a piece of land in Huangzhou purchased by Ma Mengde 馬夢得 (then serving as Huangzhou tongpan 黃州通判, Commissioner of Huangzhou Prefecture; b. 1037, a good friend of Su Dongpo. Both were born in the same year; and Ma presented the plot of ground as a gift to Su.

52. "Spring saunter"

- Written in 1082
- 8 lines, 7 characters per line
- Title in Chinese: Zhengyue ershi ri, yu Pan, Guo er sheng chu jiao xun chun, hu ji qunian shiri tong zhi Nüwangcheng zuo shi, nai he qian yun

1. The Chinese title explained: On the 20th day of the first month, together with two friends Pan Bing and Guo Gou going out to city outskirts, seeking after spring saunter. Suddenly remembered exactly this day of last year, also arriving Nüwangcheng Castle (See also poem #50).
2. Lines 3 & 4: "人似秋鴻來有信 Ren si qiuhong lai you xin, 事如春夢了無痕 Shi ru chunmeng liao wu hen" are among the most often-quoted lines from Su Dongpo's poems.
3. Zhao hun 招魂: an ancient poem in the "Chu Ci 楚辭 (Songs of Chu)" for calling home the soul of one who has died far away.

53. "Rain and the Cold Food Festival (1st of 2)"

- Written in 1082

257

- 12 lines, 5 characters per line
- Title in Chinese: Hanshi yu er shou (qi yi)

1. Cold Food (Hanshi 寒食) Festival (a 3-day cultural holiday around the Qingming Festival of April 5).
2. "Hanshitie 寒食帖": http://zh.wikipedia.org/wiki/ 寒食帖 This calligraphic masterpiece (scroll) of Su's own writing out of these two "Hanshi" poems is in the collection of Taiwan's National Palace Museum in Taipei.
3. Haitanghua 海棠花, cherry-apple or *Malus spectabilis*.

54. "Chinese flowering cherry-apple"

- Written in 1084
- 4 lines, 7 characters per line
- Title in Chinese: Haitang

1. Haitang (cherry-apple), see also poem #53.

55. "First time into Lu Mountain (3rd of 3)"

- Written in 1084
- 4 lines, 5 characters per line
- Title in Chinese: Chu ru Lushan san shou (qi san)

1. Lushan 盧山, Lu Mountain or Mount Lu, a famous mountain retreat and later resort near Jiujiang 九江 in present-day Jiangxi Province. It neighbors Poyang Lake (鄱陽湖) to the east and the Yangtze River to the north.

56. "Inscription for the wall at Westwood Temple near Lu Mountain"

- Written in 1084
- 4 lines, 7 characters per line
- Title in Chinese: Ti Xilin bi

1. Xilin referring to Xilinsi 西林寺 (Westwood Temple), in Lu Mountain 廬山. It was built in 377 by Priest Huiyong 惠永 or 慧永, 332-414.
2. This is one of the best-known and most popular poems of Su Dongpo.

57. "Japanese camellias at Fanxing Temple"

- Written in 1084
- 4 lines, 7 characters per line
- Title in Chinese: Shaobo Fanxingsi shancha

1. Fanxingsi 梵行寺 (Hindu-Brahman-Practice) Temple in Shaobo(zhen) 邵伯鎮 Township (in Yangzhou 揚州, in present-day Jiangsu Province).

58. "The fisherman (2nd of 4)"

- Written in 1085
- 5 lines, 3/3/6/7/6 characters per line
- Title in Chinese: Yufu si shou (qi er)

1. This unusual 3/3/6/7/6 characters per line format makes it a "humoresque type."

59. "Poem on a fan painting"

- Written in 1087
- 4 lines, 7 characters per line
- Title in Chinese: Shu huangqin huashan

1. Huangqin 皇親, a member of imperial household.
2. Jiangnan 江南 (River south), the Yangtze River Delta. See also poem #27.
3. Wuhu (sihai) 五湖 (四海), (Literally "five lakes and four seas"), meaning: A string of lakes along the lower Yangtze Delta and beyond or "all corners of the land." See also poem #43.
4. Wuhuxin 五湖心, as a phrase can also be interpreted as: the intention to retire and fade away.

60. "To my brother, at the New Year (3rd of 3)"

- Written in 1088
- 4 lines, 7 characters per line
- Title in Chinese: He Ziyou chuye yuanri xingsu zhizhai san shou (qi san)

1. Chuye yuanri 除夜元日, Lunar new year's eve and Lunar new year's day.
2. Xingsu zhizhai 省宿致齋, a ritual of critical self-examination and extended fasting.
3. Chunwei 春闈, or huishi 會試, referring to the provincial level of the imperial examination.

61. "On a landscape painting (1st of 2)"

- Written in 1088
- 4 lines, 7 characters per line
- Title in Chinese: Wang Jinqing suocang zhuoseshan er shou (qi yi)

1. Wang Shen 王詵, courtesy name Wang Jinqing 王晉卿, 1036-ca. 1093, poet, painter, and calligrapher.
2. The painting "zhuoseshan 著色山 (Landscape scroll in color)" was in the possession of Wang Jinqing.
3. Yingqiu 營丘 (modern Zibo 淄博, in present-day Shandong Province), is the birthplace of the well-known artist Li Cheng 李成 (919-967), who was said to have painted mountains like clouds. It is doubtful that any authentic paintings by him survive, though there are a handful of Song or Yuan dynasty paintings attributed to him.
4. Wang Shen, married to a princess, was promoted to the rank of "Zuowei jiangjun 左衛將軍" as a general in the royal guard.
5. There are two, if not three, landscape paintings attributed to Wang Shen in the Shanghai Museum. He was known for painting almost dreamlike landscapes.

62. "At Spirit Mountain, touring with friends in rain"

- Written in 1089
- 4 lines, 7 characters per line
- Title in Chinese: Tong Qin Zhong erzi yuzhong you baoshan

1. Qin Zhong 秦仲 referring to Qin Gou 秦覯, courtesy name Qin Shaozhang 秦少章 (fl. 1089), younger brother of poet Qin Guan 秦觀 (1049-1100) and Zhong Tiankuang 仲天貺 (fl. 1089).
2. Baoshan 寶山, literally "treasure mountain," meaning a mountain of religious significance and spirit.

63. "Savoring wine, on the lake, in the rain"

- Written in 1089
- 4 lines, 7 characters per line
- Title in Chinese: Yu Mo tongnian yuzhong yin hushang

1. Mo Junchen 莫君陳, fl. 1073; Tongnian 同年: colleagues of the same class, candidates who passed the imperial examination in the same year.
2. West Lake (Xi Hu 西湖) of Hangzhou 杭州, in present-day Zhejiang Province. See also poems #12,15,19.
3. Tiaozhu 跳珠, jumping pearls, implying sizable beads of raindrops.

64. "Sightseeing at Tiger Hill (2nd of 3)"

- Written in 1089
- 4 lines, 7 characters per line
- Title in Chinese: Ci yun Wang Zhongyu you Huqiu jueju san shou (qi er)

1. Wang Yu 王瑜, courtesy name Wang Zhongyu 王忠玉, fl. 1082-1099.
2. Huqiu 虎丘 Tiger Hill, a scenic district of Suzhou 蘇

州 in present-day Jiangsu Province and a famous tourist destination.

3. Qinggai 青蓋: During the Song dynasty an aristocratic style indigo blue top-cover of umbrella was primarily reserved for the prime minister to use.

4. Xiaocao 小草: Literally small grass (script), meaning manuscripts, or small ordinary scraps of writing.

5. Xuanquan 玄泉 or 懸泉, hanging springs of waterfalls.

6. Zhenniang 真娘, referring to Hu Ruizhen 胡瑞珍 (fl. 755-763), a beautiful hostess of an entertainment house during the Tang dynasty.

65. "Saying goodbye to two visitors (3rd of 5)"

• Written in 1090
• 4 lines, 6 characters per line
• Title in Chinese: Zhong Tiankuang, Wang Yuanzhi zi Meishan lai jian yu Qiantang, liu bansui, ji xing, zuo jueju wu shou song zhi (qi san)

1. Zhong Tiankuang 仲天貺, fl. 1089.

2. Wang Zhen 王箴, courtesy name Wang Yuanzhi 王元直, fl. 1090, younger brother of Su Dongpo's second wife Wang Runzhi 王閏之 (1048-1093).

3. Meishan 眉山 (in present-day Sichuan Province), hometown of Su Dongpo. Qiantang 錢塘, former name of Hangzhou 杭州 (in present-day Zhejiang Province).

4. San ren 三人, three young fellows, referring to Zhong Tiankuang, Wang Yuanzhi, and Qin Shaozhang 秦少章 (Qin Gou 秦觀, courtesy name Qin Shaozhang, fl. 1089. See also poem #62). They used to study and travel together as a group.

5. Jingkou 京口, modern Zhenjiang 鎮江 (in present-day Jiangsu Province).
6. This is an unusual format of 6-character lines.

66. "At the pavilion in the compound"

- Written in 1090
- 8 lines, 7 characters per line
- Title in Chinese: Shouxingyuan Hanbixuan

1. Shouxingyuan 壽星院 (God of Longevity Compound), in Hangzhou.
2. Hanbixuan 寒碧軒 (Cold Jasper Pavilion), a structure in the compound.
3. Xiadian 夏簟, fine bamboo splint mats for summer season.
4. Jueli 絕粒, stop eating grain, fasting.

67. "To match a poem by a friend"

- Written in 1090
- 4 lines, 7 characters per line
- Title in Chinese: You he Jingwen yun

1. Jingwen 景文, i.e. Liu Jingwen 劉景文, courtesy name of Liu Jisun 劉季孫, 1033-1092.

68. "Another quatrain"

- Written in 1090

- 4 lines, 7 characters per line
- Title in Chinese: Jueju

1. An alternate title called "Xihu jueju 西湖絕句" (West Lake Quatrain).

69. "Poem for Liu"

- Written in 1090
- 4 lines, 7 characters per line
- Title in Chinese: Zeng Liu Jingwen

1. Liu Jingwen 劉景文, see also poem #67. Liu was a colleague of Su Dongpo in Hangzhou. At the time of Su's writing the poem, Liu already had six older brothers who predeceased him. Su specifically wrote this poem to comfort and encourage him.
2. Qingyugai 擎雨蓋, raindrop-holding covers, i.e. large lotus leaves.

70. "Rhymed to match Yang's plum poem (8th of 10)"

- Written in 1091
- 4 lines, 7 characters per line
- Title in Chinese: Zai he Yang Gongji meihua shi jue (qi ba)

1. Yang Gongji 楊公濟, courtesy name of Yang Pan 楊蟠, ca. 1017-1106.
2. Meiyu 梅雨, plum rain, i.e. the East Asian rainy season, about the time of the summer solstice.

71. "Poem on Wang's paintings (4th of 4)"

- Written in 1091
- 4 lines, 7 characters per line
- Title in Chinese: You shu Wang Jinqing hua si shou: Xisai fengyu (qi si)

1. Wang Jinqing 王晉卿, courtesy name of Wang Shen 王詵, 1036-ca. 1093, a Song dynasty painter; see also poem #61.
2. Xisai 西塞, i.e. Xisaishan 西塞山 (Xisai Mountain), in Huzhou 湖州, on the south shore of Taihu Lake (太湖) in present-day Zhejiang Province.
3. Ruoli 箬笠, a conical bamboo hat.
4. Suoyi 蓑衣, rain-cloak of rushes or coir.

72. "Early morning departure, Huai River"

- Written in 1092
- 4 lines, 7 characters per line
- Title in Chinese: Huaishang zao fa

1. Huaihe River (淮河, Huai River): a major river in present-day Anhui and Jiangsu Provinces, in between the Yellow River and the Yangtze River valleys.
2. Jianghu 江湖: rivers and lakes, a term used here to imply "all corners of the country that are away from the imperial court and officialdom."
3. Shi wanglai 十往來: Ten times passing through the Huai River region during Su Dongpo's life (from 1071 to 1092).

73. "Reading Tao Yuanming on 'Drinking Wine' (15th of 20)"

- Written in 1092
- 10 lines, 5 characters per line
- Title in Chinese: He Tao yinjiu ershi shou bingxu (qi shiwu)

1. Tao 陶, i.e. Tao Yuanming 陶淵明, 365–427, also known as Tao Qian or T'ao Ch'ien 陶潛, was a Chinese poet who lived in the middle of the Six Dynasties period (222-589). Tao is often regarded as the greatest poet of the Six Dynasties period, which occurred between the Han and Tang dynasties. He is also regarded as the foremost of the "recluse" poets.
2. Liu nanzi 六男子: six young men, including Su Dongpo's three sons, and his younger brother Su Zhe's three sons.

74. "Planting pines with Du Yu (1st of 2)"

- Written in 1092
- 4 lines, 7 characters per line
- Title in Chinese: Yu shaonian po zhi zhong song, shou zhi shu wan zhu, jie zhongliangzhu yi. Duliangshan zhong jian Du Yu xiucai, qiu xue qi fa, xi zeng er shou (qi yi)

1. Du Yu 杜輿, fl. 1092, courtesy name Du Zishi 杜子師, of Xuyi 盱眙 (in present-day Jiangsu Province, close to Anhui Province), a friend of Su Dongpo.
2. Duliangshan 都梁山, Duliang Mountain, in Du Yu's hometown Xuyi.
3. Chiwu chengnan Du 尺五城南杜: an allusion "Chengnan Wei Du, qutian chiwu" (城南韋杜, 去天尺

五), implying privileged families with a close connection to the powerful imperial court.

75. "Imperial wine party (1st of 3)"

- Written in 1093
- 4 lines, 7 characters per line
- Title in Chinese: Shangyuan shiyin loushang san shou cheng tonglie (qi yi)

1. Shangyuan 上元, Lantern Festival, Lunar first month 15th day.
2. Jianzhang, i.e. Jianzhanggong 建章宮, a Han-dynasty palace, symbolizing imperial palaces of all eras.
3. Tongmingdian 通明殿 (Perspicuous Illumination Palace) refers to the court of the legendary Jade Emperor.
4. Hongyun 紅雲 (Red cloud), Yu Huang 玉皇 (Jade Emperor): One of the legends about "Yu Huang" was that he was concealed by red clouds to prevent ordinary mortals from clearly seeing him.

76. "Parting from my brother in the rain"

- Written in 1093
- 16 lines, 5 characters per line
- Title in Chinese: Dongfu yuzhong bie Ziyou

1. Dongfu 東府, another name for Song dynasty's Shangshusheng 尚書省 (Department of State Affairs), at the time brother Su Zhe was serving in that department.
2. Wutong 梧桐, Chinese parasol tree (*Firmiana simplex*).

3. Ruyin 汝陰, in Yingzhou 潁州, now Fuyang 阜陽 in present-day Anhui Province.
4. Guangling 廣陵, i.e. Yangzhou 揚州, in present-day Jiangsu Province.
5. Zhongshan 中山 now Dingzhou 定州, in present-day Hebei Province.

77. "Prompted by a memory"

- Written in 1094
- 4 lines, 7 characters per line
- Title in Chinese: Yu qianhou shou, cui Yuhang, fan wunian. Xiaqiu zhi jian, zhengre buke guo. Du Zhonghetang dongnan jia, xia kan haimen, dong shi wanli, sanfu chang xiaoran ye. Shaosheng yuannian liuyue, zhou xing fu lingwai, re shen. Hu yi cichu, er zuo shi shi

1. A unique, lengthy title of 61 characters for a poem of 28 characters. In it, the poet is telling the story of his life.
2. Yuhang 餘杭, now Hangzhou 杭州, in present-day Zhejiang Province.
3. Zhonghetang 中和堂 (The Hall of the Golden Mean), in the environs of West Lake, Hangzhou.

78. "Rhyming with Tao Yuanming (1st of 4)"

- Written in 1097
- 8 lines, 4 characters per line
- Title in Chinese: He Tao Tingyun si shou bing yin (qi yi)

1. Unusual 4-character per line poem.

2. Tao 陶, i.e. Tao Yuanming 陶淵明 (365-427). See also poem #73.

3. "Tingyun 停雲" (Unmoving clouds. To stay the clouds, implying to think of a friend or family member), a set of poems composed by Tao Yuanming.

79. "Thinking about my brother"

- Written in 1097
- 8 lines, 7 characters per line
- Title in Chinese: Shieryue shiqiri ye zuo da xiao, ji Ziyou

1. Leizhou biejia 雷州別駕, deputy magistrate of Leizhou (Su Zhe's official position at the time). Leizhou, a county in southern peninsula of present-day Guangdong Province.

80. "A favorite dish, my son's creation"

- Written in 1098
- 4 lines, 7 characters per line
- Title in Chinese: Guozi hu chu xinyi, yi shanyu zuo yusangeng, se xiang wei jie qijue. Tianshang sutuo ze buke zhi, renjian jue wu ci wei ye

1. Guozi 過子 (Guo, my son), Su Dongpo's third son Su Guo 蘇過 (1072-1123).

2. Yusangeng 玉糁羹, literally, precious as jade rice-gruel mixed with meat broth. Su Guo's new idea was to use potato instead of rice.

3. Sutuo 酥陀, a flaky baked delicacy.

4. Jinjikuai 金虀膾, literally, golden minced leek with hashed fish.

81. "A weary night"

- Written in 1099
- 8 lines, 5 characters per line
- Title in Chinese: Juanye

1. Luowei 絡緯, i.e. Fangzhiniang 紡織娘 or spinning-woman cicada (*Mecopoda elongate*), whose buzzing resembles the sound of the spinning wheel.

82. "Rhyming with Ziyou, for our friend Wu (2nd of 2)"

- Written in 1100
- 4 lines, 7 characters per line
- Title in Chinese: Ci yun Ziyou zeng Wu Ziye xiansheng er jueju (qi er)

1. Ziyou 子由, i.e. Su Dongpo's younger brother Su Zhe 蘇轍.
2. Wu Ziye 吳子野, courtesy name of Wu Fugu 吳復古, 1004-1101, a friend of Su Dongpo and Su Zhe.
3. Jiang ling 江令, Magistrate Jiang. Jiang Zong 江總 (519-594) was a Shangshuling (尚書令 Minister of Shangshusheng 尚書省); hence he was nicknamed "Jiang ling" (implying a typical government official).
4. Xie jia 謝家, The Xie clan was a powerful political family during the Eastern Jin dynasty (317-420) (implying families of high social position).

5. Jiankang 建康, national capital of the Eastern Jin dynasty, now Nanjing 南京 in present-day Jiangsu Province.

83. "Seeking lodging on a rainy night at Pure Life Monastery"

- Written in 1100
- 4 lines, 7 characters per line
- Title in Chinese: Yuye su Jingxingyuan

1. Jingxingyuan 淨行院 (Jingxingyuan, Pure Life Monastery), in Suixi County 遂溪縣 in present-day Guangdong Province.
2. Mangxie 芒鞋, straw sandals. To wear cheap straw sandals implies leading a frugal, simple life.
3. Our book title was selected from third line of this poem: "林下對牀聽夜雨 Linxia duichuang ting yeyu" (here under groves of trees / face to face in the bedroom / listening all night to the rain).

84. "Flowering plums among mountains"

- Written in 1101
- 4 lines, 7 characters per line
- Title in Chinese: Zeng ling shang mei

1. This "ling 嶺" (mountain range) referring to Dayuling 大庾嶺, one of the five ranges of Lingnan Mountains, along the border between Guangdong and Jiangxi Provinces.
2. Su was passing through this area, Qianzhou 虔州 (now Dayuxian 大余縣, in present-day Jiangxi Province), on his way back to north from his assigned exile in remote

southern island of Hainan (海南).

3. Huangmei 黃梅, plums turning ripe and golden around the lunar fourth and fifth months during the rainy season.

85. "Rhymed with Fazhi, after an old poem"

- Written in 1101
- 4 lines, 7 characters per line
- Title in Chinese: Ci yun Fazhi ju jiushi yi shou

1. Fazhi (Chanshi) 法芝 (禪師), Priest Fazhi, aka Tanxiu 曇秀, original surname Qian 錢, (fl. 1065-1101), a friend of Su Dongpo.
2. Here the term "laoshi 老師" (master) implying a respectful Buddhist monk.
3. Weng 甕, earthenware water jar. In Buddhist doctrine, when facing a water-jar full of clear water, one will be able to see into other people's minds; implied is that all people are inter-connected.

86. "Palindrome style (1st of 3)"

- Undated
- 4 lines, 7 characters per line
- Title in Chinese: Fu Jiangnan ben zhijintu shang huiwen yuanzuo san shou (qi yi)

1. Zhijintu 織錦圖, a painting of elaborate embroidery.
2. Huiwen 回文 or 迴文 denotes a palindrome in that a word, phrase, number, or other sequence of characters reads the same backward or forward.

3. Tong 桐, Tung tree (*Vernica fordii*).

87. "Baby's first bath"

- Written in probably 1084
- 4 lines, 7 characters per line
- Title in Chinese: Xier xizuo

1. Obviously this poem is a satire, referring to his unfortunate career.
2. Xier(li) 洗兒禮, a ritual of baby's first bath three days after the birth.

88. "In my dream"

- Undated
- 4 lines, 7 characters per line
- Title in Chinese: Meng zhong jueju

1. Qiushu 楸樹, *Catalpa bungei*, commonly known as Manchurian catalpa, is a species of catalpa native to China.
2. Chiri 遲日, literally "slow and dilatory days," referring to warm spring days.

89. "Spring night pleasures"

- Undated
- 4 lines, 7 characters per line
- Title in Chinese: Chunye

1. Chunye 春夜, spring night. Spring season, in classical Chinese poetics, often implies sensual desires.
2. The first line "春宵一刻 Chunxiao yike ..." is frequently recited in popular culture.

90. "Moon-Water Temple"

- Undated
- 4 lines, 7 characters per line
- Title in Chinese: Shuiyuesi

1. Shuiyuesi 水月寺, Water-Moon Temple, located in Hangzhou, in present-day Zhejiang Province.
2. Biluo 薜蘿: 薜荔 bili (*Ficus pumila*, creeping fig) and 女蘿 nüluo (*Cuscuta*, dodder, lichens) both refer to the rustic clothing of hermits.
3. Tiyunling 梯雲嶺, Ladder-step Clouds Mountain range, located in Hangzhou, Zhejiang Province.
4. Guiying 桂影, shadow of the moon, moonlight.

91. "Teasing the priest"

- Undated
- 4 lines, 7 characters per line
- Title in Chinese: Xi da Foyin

1. Foyin 佛印, Priest Foyin, original name Lin Liaoyuan 林了元, 1032-1098, a good friend of Su Dongpo.
2. Yuan-gong 遠公 refers to Priest Huiyuan 慧遠, original family name Jia 賈, 334-416, of the Eastern Jin dynasty (317-420), who established a Buddhist community on

Mt. Lu (see poem #55).

3. Tao Qian, 陶潛, better known as Tao Yuanming, 365–427, Chinese poet of the Eastern Jin dynasty (317-420); see poems #9, #73, and #78.

4. Zizhan 子瞻, Zizhan is the courtesy name of Su Dongpo.

5. Su Dongpo borrows last two lines (採得百花 Cai de baihua … & 不知辛苦 Buzhi xinku …) from a late Tang poet Luo Yin's 羅隱 (833-910) poem entitled "蜂 Feng (honey bees)."

92. "Title lost (2nd of 3)"

• Undated
• 4 lines, 6 characters per line
• Title in Chinese: Shiti san shou (qi er)

1. Unusual 6-character per line poem.
2. Handan 邯鄲, a famous historical city in present-day Hebei Province; it implies an old hometown.

93. "Song of the windlass"

• Undated
• 14 lines: 10 lines of 7-character per line; plus 4 lines of 3-character per line
• Title in Chinese: Lulu ge

1. The authorship of this poem was also credited to Tang poet Gu Kuang 顧況, ca. 725-ca. 820.
2. Yaojing 瑤井, Yaojing (Precious jade well) constellation.
3. Yusheng 玉繩, Yusheng (Jade string) constellation.

94. "Sent to a friend on an autumn day"

- Undated; (attribution questioned)
- 4 lines, 7 characters per line
- Title in Chinese: Qiuri ji youren

  1. The authorship of this poem has also been credited to Northern Song dynasty (960-1127) poet Zhang Yong 張詠, 946-1015.

95. "Mountain village (1st of 2)"

- Undated
- 8 lines, 5 characters per line
- Title in Chinese: Shancun er shou (qi yi)

  1. Title "Shancun 山村" may also be called "Jiangcun 江村."

96. "Fragments"

- Undated
- 4 lines, 5 characters per line
- Title in Chinese: Shi si ju

  1. The title reads differently in other editions:
  (1) 題陳公園二首 (Ti Chengongyuan er shou), or
  (2) 題銅陵陳公園雙池詩 (Ti Tongling Chengongyuan shuangchi shi).

CPSIA information can be obtained
at www.ICGtesting.com
Printed in the USA
BVHW081033071221
623414BV00009B/370/J